Conversations
with the Crucified

✳ REID ISAAC

Conversations with the Crucified

THE SEABURY PRESS · NEW YORK

For Sherry
who bore her own cross
with special grace
and loved me
for better, for worse

1982
The Seabury Press
815 Second Avenue
New York, N.Y. 10017

Library of Congress Cataloging in Publication Data
Isaac, Reid.
 Conversations with the crucified.
1. Jesus Christ — Crucifixion — Meditations.
I. Title.
BT450.I8   232.9'63   82–765
ISBN 0–8164–2417–9   AACR2

Note to the Reader
Some biblical references are to the Revised Standard
Version of the Bible. Old Testament Section, copyright ©
1952; New Testament Section, First Edition, copyright ©
1946; Second Edition © 1971 by Division of Christian
Education of the National Council of Churches of
Christ in the United States of America.
Grateful acknowledgment is made to the following publishers for
permission to use the materials listed:

Excerpts from the New English Bible © The Delegates of the
Oxford University Press and The Syndics of the Cambridge
University Press 1961, 1970. Reprinted by permission.

Excerpt from "For the Time Being: A Christmas Oratorio," ©
1944 and renewed in 1972 by W.H. Auden. From *Collected
Poems by W.H. Auden*, edited by Edward Mendelson. Reprinted
by permission of Random House, Inc.

Excerpt from "Ash Wednesday" in *Collected Poems 1909–1962 by
T.S. Eliot,* © 1936 by Harcourt Brace Jovanovich, Inc.; © 1963,
1964 by T.S. Eliot. Reprinted by permission of Harcourt Brace
Jovanovich, Inc. and Faber and Faber, Ltd.

"Such was the brief, such was the lonely life," from "Meditation
for a Young Boy Confirmed" by Alan Paton. Copyright © 1955
by Alan Paton. Reprinted with the permission of Charles Scrib-
ner's Sons.

Contents

Preface

> In the cross of Christ I glory,
> Towering o'er the wrecks of time;
> All the light of sacred story
> Gathers round its head sublime.

This verse from one of the hymns I sang vigorously as a young Methodist, makes the death of Jesus Christ on the cross central to the Christian's sacred story. The story of creation, the ethical teachings, the glory of the resurrected Christ, the action of God in human history make no sense without this center piece. Interpretations of the cross ranged from Jesus' blood washing away my sins to Jesus as the young and fearless prophet who stood with "humble courage for truth with heart uncowed" and still summoned me to serve humanity. No matter what the interpretive metaphor, it was always clear in the tradition of my youth, that the meaning of the cross had to be, finally, a personal one. It was not enough to understand the cross as some metaphysical transaction which balanced the scales of divine justice, or as a cosmic battle between God and the devil for the souls of human beings. The cross outside Jerusalem was meant to have some connection with the cross in my own experience and the cross at the heart of life.
Another hymn put it:

> At the cross, at the cross
> Where I first saw the light
> And the burden of my heart rolled away,
> It was there by faith I received my sight,
> And now I am happy all the day.

The vision of the cross was to send forth a light which would lighten (in both senses) the darkness of the world and the darkness of my heart.

All my life I have been intermittently attracted to religious stories that play down the dark side of life and invite me to focus on strength, courage, beauty, and peace. However, my pastoral experience as an Episcopal priest convinced me that the questions posed by life's pains and disappointments, and the intractability of evil in the world, most surely lead people to look for something or someone outside themselves to make sense out of existence.

I will never forget a conversation between a Catholic husband and his Protestant wife who was dying of cancer. She cried out: "Why does God let this happen to me?" and he said gently, "But Claire, he let it happen to his own son." Cancer is only one of the realities that show us the inadequacy of our too sunny faiths. As our optimism about human potential, both personal and social, runs into the cold wind of diminishing economic expectations and the failure of our efforts at self-fulfillment through self-affirmation, we will be more open to religious symbols that speak of the realities of limitation and loss, and life within and beyond them. The cross is the primary symbol Christianity offers to help us understand, and cope with, these trials.

In *Conversations with the Crucified* I hope to present an alternative to the pain-denying, positive-thinking faiths, both eastern and western, that have been so popular of late, as well as an alternative to the newer versions of substitutionary atonement which underlies so much of the revitalized fundamentalism we see on TV. I would like readers to find the crucified Jesus a companion in their struggles, one who helps them bear the suffering of their own lives, particularly the loss of meaning and sense of abandonment that so many of us feel these days.

A theological archeologist working on these pages could, I suspect, identify many strata of overlay to the Methodist pietism of the hymns I have recalled. One might find in the second stratum a touch of Richard and Reinhold Niebuhr, more than a touch of Tillich, some psychotherapy, as well as shadows from Ellul.

In the second, third, and fourth chapters, I am dependent almost entirely on Jürgen Moltmann's *The Crucified God.* In it, he has set forth, for me, the meaning of the cross with just the right combination of Biblical historical criticism, Trinitarian theology, and awareness of what he calls the "demonic crisis" in our society, and more importantly, hope. At the conclusion of his introduction he says: "The symbol of the cross invites rethinking. And this book is not meant to bring the discussion to a dogmatic conclusion but to be like a symbol, an invitation to thought and rethinking."[1] I have accepted his invitation and in three chapters tried to summarize my understanding of his position in a way that will make it accessible to the reader who has no training in theology. I am sure I have oversimplified what he has to say and thereby distorted it. I am sorry for that, but I have found the ore dug from his mine exceedingly rich and simply want to share some of the nuggets I found there. For those who prefer their theology straight, I recommend the Moltmann volume.

In Chapter 6, "Crucified Messiah: Living Lord," I am dependent on a series of lectures presented by Professor Clifford Stanley, of the Virginia Theological Seminary, as part of the *Christianity and Modern Man* series at the Washington Cathedral in 1953. Nothing I have heard or read has so shaped my understanding of the Bible and, particularly, the resurrection.

In the meditations of the Gospel of St. John I am obviously dependent on Raymond Brown's two-volume commentary.[2] The difference in tone between the first three Gospels and the Gospel of John makes it difficult to treat them in the same manner. The importance of the differences I found are described in a short introduction to the Johannine section.

While the first part of the book attempts to set forth a theological statement about the cross, the second and third parts are more reflective and personal. I have turned my meditation on the texts of the passion narratives into conversations with Jesus and other characters who appear there. The partners in the conversation are both biblical characters and contemporary people, speaking out of today's experience. While they are not all my own experiences, they are close enough to issues in my personal life to be available to me. It is clear that these responses to the passion of two thousand years ago are from the imagination of a middle-aged, middle-class, white American male. That is not a popular perspective at the moment, but it is the only one I have. Knowing I have not seen the universal truth, I hope the truths I have seen will be universal enough to connect with those of different experience and background.

Most of the problems and questions raised in the reflective section are left open-ended on purpose. While it may seem that the contemporary persons in these pages never get relieved of their predicaments, I have chosen to leave a lot unresolved because I believe the issues being dealt with can only finally be resolved by each of us in his own conversations with the Crucified and in a life lived in response to Him. Since most of these meditations were first prepared to be presented on Good Friday, it seemed inappropriate to move quickly to the resurrection. That is an experience given to those willing to live the pain. I hope it is given to you.

WE PROCLAIM CHRIST CRUCIFIED

All I care for is to know Christ,
to experience the power of his resurrection,
and to share his sufferings,
in growing conformity with his death,
if only I may finally arrive at the resurrection
from the dead.

Philippians 3:10–11 NEB

The Puzzle of the Cross

Have you ever gazed at a lotus blossom floating effortlessly on a quiet pond, its curved opening petals reaching upward with dazzling color in its center and soft pollen on crowds of stamen that disappear into its mysterious depth?

Eastern forms of meditation suggest we hold that image of the lotus in our minds and see it shining with light. Such contemplation holds out the promise of unity with all being. Life, light, vitality, but above all, peace, are to be found in such contemplation. You are there. The flower is there. The flower is carried on the sustaining water, you are carried on the stream of Being. Unity, peace, tranquility — these are the experiences associated with the contemplation of one of the symbols of Eastern piety — the lotus.

Contemplation of the central symbol of Christianity, the cross, is a different kind of experience. When you look at the cross on most Christian altars, you see two gold bands, covered with etched roses and joined with a monogram at the center, intersecting. Looked at with partially closed eyes, the cross resembles a broad gold ribbon surrounding a package which contains a gift.

But open your eyes, strip off the etched roses, turn the brass into two large wooden beams, nail a human body to it and watch it bleed and convulse in pain. Place around it a crowd of jeering soldiers and condemning priests. Place over it a dark cloud that hides the face of God. What mixture of feelings and thoughts come from that picture? Where is its promise of peace? In what way can this be for you a path toward unity with God?

St. Paul could look at that picture and write with enthusiasm: "Jews call for miracles, Greeks look for wisdom; but we proclaim Christ — yes, Christ nailed to the cross; and though this is a stumbling-block to Jews and folly to Greeks, yet to those who have heard his call, Jews and Greeks alike, he is the power of God and the wisdom of God." (I Corinthians 1: 22–24 NEB)

Paul looked at Jesus of Nazareth dying on the cross and saw one who set him free.

In trying to make sense, internal sense, of this picture today, we have to understand what the cross meant when it happened, twenty centuries ago. And then we have to look at our own lives, as twentieth-century human beings searching for hope and meaning in our world, to see how this grisly symbol can set us free and bring us peace.

At first it seems unlikely. The cross is offensive to the non-Christian or the atheist who cannot understand how Christians have learned to live with it so comfortably. To Israel, a person executed by crucifixion was cursed by God. "Cursed is everyone that hangs on a tree." (Deuteronomy 21:23)

To the humanist of antiquity the veneration of the crucified Jesus was embarrassing. Crucifixion was a punishment for escaped slaves and rebels against the Roman Empire. A religion with the cross at its center was unaesthetic, unrespectable, and perverse. In the human search for the good, the true, and the beautiful, the crucified Christ was not an attractive symbol.

Faith in the crucified Christ was, and is, a contradiction to all human conceptions of righteousness, beauty, and morality. The crucified God is a contradiction of everything we have ever meant, desired, and sought to be assured of by the term God. We associate the word *God* with ideas of permanence, power, beauty, and peace, not agony, punishment, blood, and death.

How do we make sense out of this different way of understanding the reality of God? If the whole Christian story is somehow gathered up in this symbol, how do we interpret it? There have been many different attempts in Christian history to explain how the cross saves us.

Recently I attended a church service in which all visitors were asked to raise their hands. The ushers then went down the aisles and handed each visitor a packet of materials which included a small pamphlet, entitled "LIFE." This pamphlet set forth an understanding of the meaning and purpose of the cross. The argument, went like this:

> We human beings have a problem.
> We are sinners, in our attitudes, thoughts, and deeds.
> Our sin is evidenced by our anxiety, fear, pride, greed, bitterness, lust, adultery, fornication, selfishness, crime, lies, cheating, etc.
> God on the other hand, is Holy and righteous.
> And *he cannot accept or have life with a person who is sinful and unrighteous.*
> God is just.
> His justice requires that he *punish every transgression of His law.*
> Every sin must be accounted for before God.
> Suppose a person sins three times a day.
> Multiplying three by 365, by your age, you will see how much you deserve God's punishment.
> *Sin must be judged* because God is a just and holy and righteous God.
> But Jesus loves us so much that He was willing to be judged and punished in our place.
> When Jesus hung upon the cross, God, the Father placed all our sins upon Him and punished Him for our sins. He punished Jesus in our place.

Jesus had no sins of his own. Jesus died to take the
punishment for our sins.
Therefore God can now accept us and love us.

(God has got rid of all the sins that deserve punishment by
beating hell out of his own son).

Because of this transaction we are assured that we are judged
innocent by God, not for the good life we have lived, but because we have identified ourselves with Jesus, God's perfect son.
He stands in for us, and puts his arm around us at the judgment
seat and says, "Let them through, they are my friends, I have
already paid the price for their admission." Without Jesus'
suffering, God would remain angry forever with his whole creation.

This way of understanding what the cross does for us has
meant a lot to many generations of Christians. It is at the heart
of the resurgent fundamentalism of our time. It lies behind the
words of Cranmer in the Rite I Eucharist in the Episcopal
Prayer Book:

All glory be to thee Almighty God, our heavenly
Father, for that thou of thy tender mercy, didst give
thine only Son Jesus Christ to suffer death upon the
cross for our redemption; who made there by his one
oblation of himself once offered, a full, perfect and
sufficient sacrifice, oblation, and satisfaction for the
sins of the whole world.

This way of understanding the meaning of the cross has great
power. It connects with something profound in the human
psyche. It cannot easily be dismissed. It may speak to some deep
need to believe that infractions of law do not go unpunished.
But the picture of God on which it is based has never been con-
vincing to me. I cannot comprehend a God who cannot accept
sinful persons without punishing someone else for his transgres-
sions. The justice of God cannot mean that God has no relation-

ship with the sinner until the sin is punished. God cannot be keeping score, three sins per day, times 365 days per year, times 45 years equals. . . .

I know that innocent people often suffer because of the sins of others. I know that I have profited by, been set free by, given life by, the sacrifices of many people, some who know and love me and some who do not know that I exist. But I cannot see why God would be willing to settle the score with me on the basis of the suffering of someone else. I would think the suffering of the most innocent person of all would only compound my guilt.

The Christian religion is based on the idea that Christ's suffering, in some way, "was for us." Something about what happened there brought life to me. But what was it? How did it work?

As sure as I know anything in this mysterious world, I know that God did not have to wait for the sacrifice of his sinless son to associate with me. I am sure God does not work that way and I find the picture offensive, because of what I have learned about God by looking at him through the lens of Jesus.

As I look at the Jesus who actually bore the cross, I see a man who reached out to the prisoners crucified with him, who had dinner with tax-collectors, who wrote in the sand while the accusers of the woman taken in adultery skulked away, who touched the unclean lepers, and who conversed with those possessed by demons. In all these actions Jesus was offering reconciliation, forgiveness, at-one-ment, to people who didn't know that was what they needed and who didn't know how to ask for it. He reached across and broke down barriers they had erected by their sins when they were too blind and too bound to change themselves.

Because of this Jesus, I can see God in no other way than as the Father of the Prodigal who runs to meet the returning son, or the shepherd who leaves the ninety and nine to find the one lost sheep, or even one who looks at the self-confident rich young ruler and loves him.

In this Jesus, the fullness of God was present. This Jesus is the image of the invisible one. The style of his life and the content of his teaching has everything to do with why and how his death sets me free and gives me life.

It is not by balancing some cosmic scale that he saves me. It is by setting loose in the world a new spirit of accepting love and a new power to overcome the deep separations of life.

I must look for the clue to its meaning for me in the events which brought about the cross two thousand years ago.

A Blasphemous Healer

Jesus of Nazareth was crucified for very specific historical reasons. To understand what the death of Jesus on the cross means to us, we have to understand what it was about his life that led to his death.

He met his death as a result of the reaction of two groups of people to his ministry. He died because his Roman and Jewish contemporaries were provoked to kill him by his own words and actions.

He was finally condemned by the Romans as a political rebel. He was condemned by his Jewish contemporaries as a blasphemer and a demagogic false Messiah. Within the world view of these two groups there was justice to both charges.

The earliest account of the charge of blasphemy being leveled against Jesus is found in the second chapter of St. Mark's Gospel:

> While he was proclaiming the message to them a man was brought who was paralyzed. Four men were carrying him, but because of the crowd they could not come near. So they opened up the roof over the place where Jesus was, and when they had broken through they lowered the stretcher on which the paralyzed man was lying. When Jesus saw their faith, he said to the paralyzed man, "My son, your sins are forgiven."
>
> (Mark 2:2-5 NEB)

Let us look closely at the words of this story.

While he was proclaiming the message . . . Mark gives us a brief summary of the message in his first chapter:

> The time has come;
> the kingdom of God is upon you;
> repent, and believe the Gospel. (Mark 1:15 NEB)

Jesus is saying, "The time of waiting is over. God's sovereign rule is on its way: God has determined the length of time that must elapse before the coming of His kingdom, and that time is now up. God is about to assert his authority and bring things into conformity with his will. There is nothing more important to do than to get yourself ready. Turn around, come to your senses, turn from your sinful past toward God. Believe that the new order is imminent and act on that belief. Claim for yourself a part in the future God is offering." There was an urgency to that message, an openness, a sense of possibility, and an excitement.

While Jesus was preaching, the four friends brought to him a man who was *paralyzed*. Think of what it means to be paralyzed and unable to move, dependent on the care of your friends. Paralysis is a physical disablility caused by damage to the blood vessels in the brain. But we also use the word to describe psychic conditions that keep us from moving.

"I was paralyzed with fear, so scared I couldn't move."

"I was paralyzed with embarrassment, I wished the earth would open up and swallow me."

"I was paralyzed by indecision. I didn't know which way to turn."

"I was paralyzed with depression. I didn't want to get up in the morning."

A man described as *paralyzed* is brought to Jesus, the hard way. A crowd is pushing around the door of the house. People, active aggressive people, are everywhere. They do not give way to let the paralyzed man in. His friends literally have to raise the roof to get attention for him.

When Jesus saw their faith, he said to the paralyzed man, "My son, your sins are forgiven." The faith Jesus saw was the faith of the four friends. They had overcome great difficulties to get their neighbor to a source of help. No discouragement turned them back. They might have come to the door and said, "Well, it's so crowded, we'd better leave and come back another time." They might have said, "We don't want to disturb the doctors and nurses and complain about the service." They might have acquiesced when told to "take a seat until the social worker can see you."

No. They are determined. They push, shove, lift, haul. They find ropes, uncover the roof, and interrupt the teaching. They make a mighty nuisance of themselves.

As he often did, Jesus interpreted this persistence — even to the point of nuisance-making — as a sign of faith. The paralytic's friends believed that if they could get him to Jesus, Jesus would heal him.

Jesus then says, *"My son, your sins are forgiven."* It may seem strange to talk about forgiveness when the man was physically ill, but in Jesus' time it was believed that illnesses were the result of invasion by a demon and/or the consequences of some sin committed by the sufferer or by his or her parents. So it was not so strange to offer forgiveness to the sick. If someone was sick, that was a sign that something was wrong that needed to be forgiven. Jesus does not ask what he has done or if he repents, Jesus simply says, "Your sins are forgiven."

Now there were some lawyers sitting there and they thought to themselves, *"Why does this fellow talk like that? This is blasphemy: Who but God alone can forgive sins?"* Only the judge has the right to forgive. Forgiveness is God's prerogative. Who is this man who arrogates it to himself?

Jesus was intervening in a matter where all rights were reserved to God alone. God would decide at some future Judgment Day who would be forgiven and who would not.

But Jesus was saying: "You don't have to wait for God's final judgment. I'll tell you, right now — You are forgiven!"

What right did he have to say this? He was only a carpenter's son. He was deifying himself by taking over God's work. This, indeed, was blasphemy. According to the religion of the time, the victory of God would come when the righteous who suffer injustice on earth were exalted and the lawless and godless put to shame. But Jesus was preaching that God's kingdom was present here and now, *not as judgment*, but as grace. He acted out this message by socializing with sinners and tax-collectors. His actions contradicted all hopes based upon being good.

Jesus' message and his style of life set him apart from John the Baptist in whose circle he had begun his ministry. He and John both preached, "The Kingdom of God is at hand." For John, God was coming as a judge to punish evil and reward the good. For Jesus, the Kingdom was present as the unconditional and free grace of God by which the lost and those without rights were sought out, and the unrighteous were accepted.

When Jesus laid claim to the grace of God for transgressors of the law, he set himself above Moses. He did not even try to support his message by appeals to the tradition of his people. His authority, he claimed, came directly from One he called "My Father." He said his Father's coming Kingdom would not bring glory to the righteous and condemnation to the unrighteous, but the reverse. The Kingdom is offered to the unrighteous as a gift of grace, and the supposedly righteous are left out of it. The scribes and lawyers whose job it was to interpret the Laws of God had good reason to protest against a God so generous to the evil doer as to undermine all authority and order. He threatened the very meaning and structure of their lives. This flabby God was not the God of the Torah.

W.H. Auden puts the natural man's protest against Jesus' God into the mouth of Herod in *A Christmas Oratorio*:

> Legislation is helpless against the wild prayer of long-ing that rises, day in, day out, from all these house-holds under my protection: "O God, put away justice and truth for we cannot understand them and do not

want them. Eternity would bore us dreadfully. Leave Thy heavens and come down to our earth of water-clocks and hedges. Become our uncle. Look after Baby, amuse Grandfather, escort Madam to the Opera, help Willy with his home-work, introduce Muriel to a handsome naval officer. Be interesting and weak like us, and we will love you as we love ourselves.". . . Justice will be replaced by Pity as the cardinal human virtue, and all fear of retribution will vanish. Every cornerboy will congratulate himself: "I'm such a sinner that God had to come down in person to save me. I must be a devil of a fellow." Every crook will argue: "I like committing crimes, God likes forgiving them. Really the world is admirably arranged.". . . Naturally this cannot be allowed to happen. Civilization must be saved even if this means sending for the military, as I suppose it does. How dreary. . . . Why couldn't this wretched infant be born somewhere else? Why can't people be sensible?. . . Why can't they see that the notion of a finite God is absurd. Because it is. . . . And for me personally at this moment it would mean that God had given me the power to destroy Himself. I refuse to be taken in.[1]

Maybe Jesus' God is not the kind of God we are looking for either. We feel impotent and weak, we want a God who will be omnipotent and strong for us. There are too many Cains killing too many Abels. We want a God who will keep law and order in the world—the sheep and the goats separated. We want a God who will protect us against the lawless, the ugly, the weak, and hateful in other people, but especially in ourselves. We will not have a God who does not judge, who is not powerful, and who is not in control. We want a God we can wrap around us so that rage and grief and pain do not touch us.

And what does Jesus offer us? He offers us a God who does not come to judge, but to offer forgiveness. He offers us a cross where he becomes weak and vulnerable, a cross where he accepts his humanity and our humanity, his mortality, and our mortality, where he opens himself to suffering and to love.

He shows us a God who allows himself to be humiliated and crucified. He breaks down all the protective walls we have erected against those who are different, those who threaten us, those who are ugly. The cross breaks through our protective apathy and calls us to a life of suffering and love. Jesus is calling us to live out the accepting love of God with the unlovely, beginning with ourselves.

Was Jesus right, or were his critics right?

The events seemed to prove Jesus wrong. The God whose gracious love he declared did not save him from the cross. He died a horrible death, condemned by those who claimed to know God best. He was an upstart, a man without authority who blasphemously presumed to act as the agent of God, with no one to back him up but his Father, who, in the end, did not.

His friends lost faith in him. They forsook him and fled, not out of cowardice, but because their faith in him died. He was wrong. God was not like what he said. The powerful and the righteous still had things under control. Jesus' gracious Father withheld his hand. Jesus was repudiated by men and by God.

Or was he?

Was this healer only the blasphemous, dead pseudo-teacher and false prophet?

When you answer that question, remember that the God who chooses to lay aside his glory and to identify with the suffering people in his world will always sound blasphemous to you if you do not want to go that way yourself.

✳ 3

A Rebel with a Human Cause

The Nicene Creed says, "He was crucified under Pontius Pilate." These words root the crucifixion of Jesus in our human history. His death was not part of a myth, a story about something that could have happened anywhere, in heaven or on earth, or not at all. Jesus of Nazareth was crucified at a particular historical moment in a particular geographical place, by a particular human ruler, because of very specific historical conflicts.

The creed does not mention that Jesus was rejected by the Jews, only that he was crucified by a Roman procurator. Jesus may have been judged a blasphemer by his own people, but he did not die the death of a blasphemer. The punishment for blasphemy was stoning. He died on a cross — the Roman instrument for dealing with escaped slaves and rebels against the state. The charge over his head was a political one, "The King of the Jews." He was crucified because Pilate concluded his presence in Jerusalem could lead to political turmoil. His entrance into the city on a colt, in a fashion which recalled Zechariah's prophecy of the coming of the King, was provocative. He turned over the temple tables of exchange, damaging other people's property, causing a ruckus at a time when the city was filled with crowds already at a pitch of religious frenzy, celebrating their liberation from Egypt.

He had gone too far.

There was a group of patriots in Israel called Zealots. They were offended by the images of Roman authority placed over the gate of their temple, and by the images of the Roman emperor imprinted on the coins they used to pay an annual head tax. Zealots called on all good Jews to resist the occupying power. "Destroy the law-breakers and cleanse Israel," they cried. Believing God's coming rule depended on the use of force to cast out the current Roman rule, some hoped Jesus was presenting himself to lead such a revolt.

Like the Zealots, Jesus preached that the Kingdom of God, the rule of God, was about to be realized. He said he had come to preach good news to the poor, to proclaim the release of the captives, to announce the year of the Lord's coming. That message would not sound nonpolitical to a Roman government that expected its empire to last forever. The Zealots, hoped Jesus might be one of them.

But Jesus was notorious as a friend of tax-collectors whom the Zealots held to be collaborators with the enemy — the most despicable of traitors. Jesus reached across political lines to embrace tax-collectors, just as he reached across racial lines to embrace Samaritans. He ate and drank and went to parties. His way of life was festive. How could he live like this, groaned the Zealots, in the face of the economic distress and political servitude of his people? Didn't he care?

Jesus cared. He condemned rulers who acted as if they were God. He pronounced woe to the rich. But he did not call on the poor to avenge themselves. He did not urge the oppressed to oppress their oppressors. He said, "If a Roman soldier asks you to carry his burden for one mile, go with him two." "If a man takes away your coat, give him your cloak also." "Love your enemies and pray for those who persecute you."

What was revolutionary about that? His call to give up the effort to establish the rule of God by force was revolutionary. His God was coming, he said, not to take revenge on evil, but to grant his grace to sinners, whether they be tax-collectors or Zealots, Pharisees or law-breakers, Jews or Samaritans, or even Roman centurions.

His rebellion was against inhumanity. He denied that any human being — Zealot or Roman — had the right to pass judgment and execute vengeance in his or her own cause. The God who was coming was incomprehensibly generous. Jesus refused to enter into the game of force vs. counter force. That was a struggle that both Zealots and Romans understood well. Jesus didn't fit in. He interfered in their business by challenging and disrupting its rules. Both sides wanted him out of the way.

His revolution called for a change in perception. He asked both Zealots and Romans to acknowledge their common humanity, their common sinfulness before God, and their common hope in God's gracious forgiveness.

Pilate seems to have concluded that Jesus was not a Zealot, but in the deeper sense it was true that his message, if accepted, would undermine the empire, as, in the end, it did. Jesus' loyalty to the rule of God brought every human absolutism into question. It surely would undercut Pax Romana.

In the first century, religion and politics were never separated. The political implications of Jesus' message were clear. The old order was coming to an end. So when he was brought before Pilate and asked if he were the "King of the Jews," he replied, "You have said so." When asked to defend himself, he did not. Then the soldiers took him and mocked him, saluted him as a King, crowned him with thorns, and knelt before him ridiculing the foolishness of his revolution.

He was crucified as a rebel against the imperial authority, as a nuisance who threatened to disturb the peace and order of the great empire. The Romans had the power. When it came right down to it, his talk about the power of God, whom he called "Father" was no match for the Roman legions.

Things were as they had always been. There was no new age coming. The prisoners were not free. The poor were still poor. The year of the Lord hadn't come. Jesus' vision of the coming

Kingdom was a dream, a fantasy. He was just one more wild fanatic to be crucified "under Pontius Pilate."

The pity was that he had led so many astray. So many had put their hopes in him and given up everything to follow him, and it had all come to naught.

They must have been crazy to believe that there was any power stronger than Rome. The world was like what the Romans and the Zealots said it was. Power was what counted. Jesus of Nazareth? "How many legions has he?" His career was just one more tempest in the ever-boiling Judean teapot. Next year there would be others, and they would be dealt with in the same way. The world does not change.

His followers, their faith destroyed by the cross, dispersed. Yet in a few weeks those frightened fishermen and tax-collectors and reformed prostitutes were back in Jerusalem declaring that there had been a great reversal. God had raised Jesus up, they said. God had overruled the judgment of Caesar's lackey. There was a higher authority than the power of the state. God had overruled the system that condemned Jesus. The rebel, the outcast, the son of the oppressed had been justified by God. God was not on the side of the political authority. God was present with the outcast and the condemned. God had remembered the rebel Jesus, as he had remembered Jonah.

Never again would the totalitarian claims of the state, any state, be taken with final seriousness. After the state gave its judgment, the ultimate judgment was in the hands of one who had overturned the judgment of the state.

So it is that the worshippers of the crucified and resurrected rebel sing the song of his mother:

> The arrogant of mind and heart he has put to route.
> He has brought monarchs from their thrones,
>   but the humble have been lifted high.
> The hungry he has satisfied with good things,
>   the rich sent empty away.

He has ranged himself at the side of Israel his servant;
    firm in his promise to our forefathers,
he has not forgotten to show mercy to Abraham
    and his children's children, for ever.
                                        (Luke 1:52–55 NEB)

Ever since then, the cross has been a sign of contradiction to the presumptive powers of this world. The cross has become a sign to which rebels have rallied across the ages.

Martin Luther King appealed from a Birmingham jail to the followers of Jesus to look beyond the authority of the law that separated black and white and claim the gracious openness of Jesus' God.

The Bishops of Uganda defied Idi Amin in the name of the crucified and risen one, and followed him to martyrdom. Dietrich Bonhoeffer and the German Christians rebelled against the authority of Hitler, and joined in the suffering of the cross of Jesus.

Alan Paton and the South African Christians say "We must obey the God of the crucified and risen rebel rather than the law of apartheid."

The Sandanistas of Nicaragua sang their songs about Jesus and the justice of his God, and overthrew the tyrant Samosa.

A group of Christians calling themselves, "The Ploughshares Eight" entered a General Electric plant in Harrisburg, Pennsylvania where components of nuclear weapons were being assembled. They smashed the instruments of death. They destroyed property which did not belong to them. The guard who arrested them said, "This time you've gone too far."

They destroyed property designed to destroy life on this earth. They asked us not to accept the reassurance of our leaders that more bombs will make us safe. Look, what you are doing, they said, before it is too late. At their trial, the judge said, "Nuclear war is not on trial here, you are."

But nuclear war should be on trial someplace.

What can be done to bring it to trial?

How far is too far, if life on this planet is at stake?

Those of us who worship the crucified and risen rebel expect the time will come when we will be asked to put our lives on the line. Will we believe that the God who raised the crucified rebel from the dead has the final word and act on that belief? Are we ready to trust that Word, even when it leads to crosses ordered by the Pilates of our time?

In our moment of history we may not be clear about the line on which we should place our lives. But if we live by faith in the Jesus who was crucified as a rebel, we know that there may be a cross for us.

As long as people are tortured and killed and maimed reaching for freedom, Jesus the crucified and risen one stands among them, the brother to all sufferers. We, his body in the world, stand with him and with them.

Where help is possible, we give it. Where no help is possible, we walk with those who are beyond help.

The God Forsaken God

The crowds that had pressed around Jesus to hear him speak, to be healed, to be fed, were gone. The disciples, those special ones with whom he had spent so much time, all had taken flight. The priests, his accusers, were there challenging him to prove he was the saviour by saving himself. The Roman soldiers, who couldn't understand what this was all about, who thought one victim was the same as another, they were there. But Jesus was dying alone.

The physical pain was awful, but there was always pain in such a death. The abuse heaped on the dying man was awful, but he had learned to live with abuse. Death was something everyone must face and he had chosen this kind of death.

The depth of his suffering did not lie in these things. The depth of it, the worst of it, the final straw, was the sudden sense that he had been abandoned by God, his Father. The only words Mark records from the cross are the despairing words from the twenty-second psalm,

> Eli, Eli, lema sabachthani, which means,
> "My God, my God, why hast thou forsaken me?"
> (Mark 15:34-5 NEB)

The deepest point in his passion was the point when he realized that God, his God, the one he called Abba, Father, the one whose gracious nearness he had proclaimed all his life, was now far from him. God had forsaken him. He was utterly alone.

How different this is from the death of Socrates. Socrates embraced his death with magnanimity and turned it into an occasion to discuss the immortality of the soul. He drank his hemlock, surrounded by his admirers, superior in every way to those who had condemned him. He faced death as he had lived — rationally, soberly, urbanely.

Jesus' death was different. He died with a loud cry. His whole message had been about the closeness of God his Father. His fellowship with God was direct and personal. He had trusted in God as no one had ever trusted before.

Now, there were no miracles, no words of approval, no doves descending. The torment in his torment was his abandonment by God. As a blasphemer, Jesus was rejected by the guardians of his people's tradition. As a rebel, he was crucified by the Romans. But finally and most profoundly, he was rejected by God his Father. The life of Jesus ends with an open question about God — Can he be trusted to watch over his own?

We resist this picture and try to interpret Jesus' cry in some way that will keep him in touch with God to the very end. Luke does not even record this cry of dereliction. Instead he has Jesus say, "Into thy hands I commit my spirit." John has him say, triumphantly, "It is finished." But Mark, and Matthew following him, make us look at a man whose assurance had deserted him. It is embarrassing to us. We do not want to watch it. Let us not linger on it. Let him hurry and finish the dying so we can get on to the resurrection.

Such moments are an embarrassment when they take place on the death bed of one of our family or friends. We say, "Poor dear, she doesn't know what she is saying." "He doesn't really mean that." So if we cannot accept the sense of abandonment of those closest to us at the time of death, how can we accept it from the one we worship as God incarnate? Surely God cannot have abandoned himself. Surely God's Son could not lose his cool, so to speak.

Jesus' cry challenges our basic assumptions about God. We have inherited, along with our Christianity, the Greek philosophical concept that God is incapable of suffering. The Godhead for the Greek needs nothing. It is a perfect being without emotions. Anger, hate, envy are all alien to it. But so are love, compassion, and mercy. A God who is subject to suffering like all other creatures, cannot be God. God is the unmoved mover drawing all things to himself, but himself drawn to nothing.

Those who worship such a God think they should be the same. Don't let yourself be influenced by outside demands. Try to develop a life which is unchangeable. Don't be too sensitive. Keep your passions under control. Overcome your needs and drives and lead a life free of trouble and anger and love. Become apathetic. That is the only way to live in a world where the gods are imperturbable.

But in the Old Testament, in the Jewish tradition, we get a different picture of God. There God is deeply affected by the events of history, by what people do or don't do. Hosea describes God longing for his child Israel who has forsaken his covenant.

> How can I give you up, Ephraim,
>   how surrender you, Israel?
>
> It was I who taught Ephraim to walk,
>   I who had taken them in my arms;
> but they did not know that I harnessed them
> in leading strings
>   and led them with bonds of love —
> that I had lifted them like a little child to my cheek,
>   that I had bent down to feed them.
>
> My heart is changed within me,
>   my remorse kindles already,
> I will not let loose my fury.... (Hosea 11:3,8-9a NEB)

God is angry with his child, Israel. His wrath is injured love. The opposite of love is not wrath, but indifference. For God to be indifferent toward the just or unjust behavior of his children would be to retreat from his promise. It would be the opposite of love.

The modern existentialist also protests against God the imperturbable unmoved mover. A God who cannot suffer and die is inferior to man. A God who is incapable of tears, who is unmoved by pain, cannot love either.

We human beings suffer because we love and we suffer to the degree that we love. If we kill all love in ourselves, we no longer suffer. We become apathetic.

What sort of Being is a God who is only Almighty? He is not God, but a stone. A God who experiences helplessness, a God who suffers because he loves, and who dies for what he loves, is more worthy of our devotion than an omnipotent God who cannot suffer, cannot love, cannot die.

The cross shows us the heart of another God, different from the powerful creator of the philosophers. In the cross we see a God who has experienced the depth of human suffering in his abandonment by what he had counted on most deeply. If God does not experience the total eclipse of meaning that we experience, he doesn't know what it is to be human, and is of no help to us.

On the other hand, if we believe that God was in Christ, entering fully into the situation of man, then he is our companion. In the person of his Son Jesus, he enters, descends, deeper and deeper, embraces it all, accepts it all, without limits and conditions. He becomes truly human.

The God we know in Jesus does not come to us as a religion which calls for religious thoughts and feelings. God does not come to us as a law, so that we participate in his life through obedience. God does not come to us as an ideal, so that we achieve community with him through constant striving. God comes to us in a God forsaken man. All of us who know we are God forsaken know that he is our companion. There is no loneliness or rejection that the crucified God has not experienced. The God forsaken and rejected (who is each of us) can accept him or herself by coming to know the crucified God who is with us and has already accepted us. God in Christ has identified with all our life, including our death.

Christ's agony would not have been as deep as ours if he could have sustained an eternal hope until the end. For God to be man, he had to lose touch with that ultimate security. Christ's cry on the cross means that God renounces his long-standing privileges and himself experiences the agony of death and the loss of meaning.

The cross is taken up by God. It is taken up into God. To be able to recognize God in the cross of Christ is to recognize the cross, death, and rejection in God, and God in all of these. The crucified Jesus is called the "image of the invisible God," which means that God is like this. God is not greater than he is in this humiliation. God is not more powerful than he is in this help-lessness. God is not more divine than he is in this humanity. The full deity of God is to be found in the final agony of the crucified Christ. Elie Wiesel tells a story about two Jewish men and a youth being executed in front of a gathering of the entire concentration camp.

> The men died quickly but the death struggle of the boy lasted for half an hour. "Where is God? Where is he?" a man behind me asked. As the boy, after a long time, was still in agony on the rope, I heard the man cry again. "Where is God now?" and I heard a voice within me answer. "Here he is. He is hanging there on this gallows!"[1]

He is hidden there
   in the one who asks the question
   in the one who dies,
   and in the one who recognizes his presence.
He is there — our divine companion.

✳ 5

The Challenge of the Innocent Victim

In Albert Camus' book, *The Plague*, a Jesuit priest, Father Paneloux, preaches two sermons to the people in the rat-infested town where many are dying painful, horrible deaths. He begins his first sermon:

> Calamity has come on you my brethren, and, my brethren, you deserved it.[1]

He continues:

> To long this world of ours has connived at evil, too long it has counted on the divine mercy, on God's forgiveness.... For a long while God gazed down on this town with eyes of compassion; but He grew weary of waiting, His eternal hope was too long deferred, and now He has turned His face away from us. And so, God's light withdrawn, we walk in darkness, in the thick darkness of this plague.[2]

During the weeks that follow, Father Paneloux works beside an unbelieving doctor friend who is caring for the dying. One day the priest stands with his friend beside a bed and watches a young boy die. Through the child's screams of agony, Father Paneloux cries "My God, spare this child."[3]

His friend, the doctor, who has never accepted the idea that the plague was the result of the town's wickedness, turns to the priest when the child dies and says, "That child, anyhow, was innocent, and you know it as well as I do!"

The priest replies, "It passes our human understanding. But perhaps we should love what we cannot understand." The doctor says, "And until my dying day I shall refuse to love a scheme of things in which children are put to torture."[4]

There are three crosses on Calvary. At the place where Jesus dies, two other men die as well. Their deaths do not move us in the same way. Although every death is a problem, and every death diminishes us and speaks to us of our own, Jesus' death on the cross troubles us more profoundly. In his death we have to come to terms with the suffering of the innocent. Though every death is a threat, the death of the man in the middle offends our sense of justice. It calls into question the rightness of the world. The death of the innocent on the cross brings to mind other innocents who have suffered. We remember Elie Wiesel's young boy, and Anne Frank, and the millions of her faith who were executed in camps, built by gentiles. The Irish or Lebanese child caught in the cross fire of adult passions, the old woman struck down by a mugger, the pilot shot by a hi-jacker, the school girl who eats a can of poisoned tuna fish — these deaths make us cry out. Why? Why? Why?

The Christian religion puts the cross on which the innocent Jesus died at the center of our worship. Year after year and week after week we are confronted by that cross with Jesus on it and the cross that appears in our daily newspaper and each one of us is asked, "What are you going to make of this?" There are three possible responses to the cross on Calvary and the crosses in human history.

I can reject the reality of the cross in order to preserve my sense of the goodness of life. I can refuse to look at the cross. I can refuse to consider the suffering of the innocent a serious problem. If this thing really happens all the time, then this world does not make sense and life in it is intolerable. I have to believe that those who rejoice, deserve to rejoice, and those who weep, deserve to weep. Therefore when I look at the man on the cross, I have to say, "If he's suffering like that, he must be guilty. A good God would not let such a thing happen unless he deserved it. If a person suffers that way, it must be because he has done something evil."

I deny the reality of the cross in order to hold on to the goodness of life, and the justice of God.

A second reaction is to accept the cross and deny the goodness of life. I accept the fact that the world is full of undeserved, useless, and purposeless suffering. Therefore, I will remain cynical about the promises of life and its relationships. The cross stands for all that is absurd and unfair in life. When I take it seriously, I cannot trust life or believe in God.

There is a third way which accepts life with the cross as part of it and the cross as part of life. Father Paneloux sees the plague finally forcing two decisions on all who are touched by it.

The first decision is whether to love God or to hate God. The blood of Christ, mingled with the blood of all innocent victims of this world's evil and accidents, cries out to hate God.

When I hear that cry, I am forced to decide to love my fate, including the cross, or to reject it, curse it, and die. I must either find a way to love the God who does not protect me from pain, or hate him. That is the first decision I have to make. No one ever makes it once and for all. It has to be made over and over again.

The second choice I have is whether to stay to the end, or to run away. In Father Paneloux's second sermon shortly before his own death, he no longer accuses. He no longer addresses his congregation as "you." He now says "we." He reminds his listeners of accounts of an earlier plague in the city of Marseille:

> If the chronicles of the Black Death at Marseille were to be trusted, only four of the eighty-one monks in the Mercy Monastery survived the epidemic. And of these four three took to flight.... Father Paneloux

had found his thoughts fixed on that monk who stayed on by himself, despite the death of his seventy-seven companions, and above all, despite the example of his three brothers who had fled. And, bringing down his fist on the edge of the pulpit, Father Paneloux cried in a ringing voice: "My brothers, each one of us must be the one who stays!"[5]

Will I be the one who watches with those who suffer, or will I be the one who goes to sleep?

Will I stand by the beds of the plague victims, or will I try to quarantine them?

Will I stay in the city where the dying is going on, or will I run? As I struggle with these two questions: to love God or to hate God, to stick it out or to run away, I look at the man on the middle cross. If I look at him long enough, I discover that there is more there than simply a symbol of injustice. For me, the man on the cross has become the giver of freedom. Killed by hatred, he is the wellspring of love. Dying he offers life. The cross suggests to me that maybe only the captive can finally end captivity. Maybe only the dying can finally conquer death. Maybe only the love that suffers evil can finally overcome evil.

Meditating on the cross is meditating on the mystery by which good and evil are eternally mixed in the world.

We are signed with the cross in our baptism and called to take up our cross daily and follow him. If we stay with the suffering of the innocent in this world, refusing to protect ourselves by denial or running away, when it comes our own time, we will discover we have a companion in our suffering. We have become brothers and sisters of the one whose cross was a victory, and out of whose death life came.

✳ 6

Crucified Messiah: Living Lord

Clifford Stanley, in his lectures on *Jesus—Fact and Faith* has described the religious encounters in the Bible in this way: "In the Biblical stories of great religious encounters there are two characteristic elements. The first is the "appearance"—i.e. God is present with a special intensity in a different way than he has appeared before. The second element in the religious encounters in the Bible is the internal conflict in the one to whom God appears."

We can see this pattern in the stories of Moses at the burning bush (Exodus 3), Isaiah in the temple (Isaiah 6), and St. Paul on the road to Damascus (Acts 9). In each of these appearances, God calls someone to a mission, and in each case the call sets off a conflict within the man. The elements are always the same, and their order is always the same: first the appearance, then the conflict. Professor Stanley suggests that the elements are right, but the order is wrong. He suggests that we can understand the nature of the religious encounter better if we reverse the order, first the conflict, then the appearance.

A person in conflict is not sure which way to turn. He is not sure who he is or what he is called to be. He is divided.

Should Moses stay in the security of his stepfather's household, or is he called to do something about the suffering of his people in Egypt?

Isaiah is divided. The king's long reign is ended. The country is in political turmoil. Does he have a word from the Lord that he should speak at this time, or should he remain a private citizen?

Paul is divided. He knows the followers of Jesus are undermining his people's understanding that they are justified by their obedience to the law and he is determined to stamp out this threat and yet he has watched Stephen die upheld by his faith in Jesus, and Paul is beginning to wonder if perhaps these heretics have hold of something he needs.

A person in conflict is not sure who he is or what he is called to do.

Uncertain about themselves, they are uncertain about God too. They are in conflict about the nature, will, and purpose of God. Which is the will of God? Which is the word of God? God seems to be on both sides, and on neither side. On which side is God going to come down?

The conflict is resolved by a decision, a decision about themselves and about who God is for this hour. The decision is a decision about God. God shows which side he is on. During the conflict, God disappears. Once it is resolved, God comes rushing back. God is now understood in a way he was never understood before.

This pattern of religious encounter in the Bible, is the key to understanding the disciples' experience of the resurrection. It is clear in Luke's description of the appearance of the risen Lord to the disciples on the road to Emmaeus.

> That same day two of them were on their way to a village called Emmaeus, which lay about seven miles from Jerusalem and they are talking together about all these happenings. As they talked and discussed it with one another, Jesus himself came up and walked along with them; but something held their eyes from seeing who it was.
> He asked them, "What is it you are debating as you walk?"

They are in conflict, they are discussing, they are debating. Something is unresolved, they are divided within themselves. Back and forth, back and forth, how to make sense out of their experience. Jesus asks them to describe their conflict to him.

> They halted, their faces full of gloom, and one, called Cleopas, answered, "Are you the only person staying in Jerusalem not to know what has happened there in the last few days?"
> "What do you mean?" he asked.
> "All this about Jesus of Nazareth," they replied, "a prophet powerful in speech and action before God and the whole people; how our chief priests and rulers handed him over to be sentenced to death, and crucified him. But we had been hoping that he was the man to liberate Israel."
>
> (Luke 24:18-22 NEB)

Jesus had been a prophet powerful in speech and action. It seemed clear that God had been with him. And yet he had been crucified. That was a contradiction. God's chosen one, if he was really chosen, could not have come to such an end. The manner of his death had constituted a great No from God. Because no one had ever heard of a Messiah, a deliverer, a liberator who had been crucified. Nothing could happen except by the will of God (for good Jews) and if God let this happen to Jesus, it must mean he was not the one they hoped for. In their tradition it was the good who prospered, and the evil who were punished. Hadn't the Psalmist said of the chosen of God, "For he has charged his angels to guard you wherever you go, to lift you on their hands for fear you should strike your foot against a stone."

> (Psalm 91:11-12 NEB)

The thieves who were crucified with him and the priests who watched it all said the same thing: "If you are the Messiah, come down from the cross." That would have been the only possible proof that God was with him. It had not happened.

That was one side of the conflict. God's Messiah does not get crucified. The other side was still there. "They had hoped he would be the one to liberate Israel." They hoped no longer, and yet they still debated. How could they have been so wrong?

It was hard to continue to believe in Jesus, and yet they couldn't give him up. If the conflict was going to be resolved, it had to be resolved on the basis of their religious tradition. If there was any way to make sense out of this paradox, they would have to find it in their scriptures. Everything they knew about God was there. It all seemed to point away from Jesus as God's chosen one.

So Jesus took them back to look at the scriptures again:

> "How dull you are!" he answered. "How slow to be-lieve all that the prophets have said! Was the Messiah not bound to suffer thus before entering upon his glory?"
> Then he began with Moses and all the prophets, and explained to them the passages which referred to himself in every part of the scriptures.
> (Luke 24:25–27 NEB)

The Gospels are full of references to verses they found which would make it intelligible to accept a crucified Messiah. Isaiah 53 and Psalm 22 are two of the most important texts, to which they turned.

But what was the religious issue in this conflict?

Everything they had known about God up to that time had been revealed through creation and through life. That is a true way of knowing God and it is important. But if the only way to know God is through creation and life: spring flowers, mighty mountains, great human characters, then when you are sick or in trouble you think you're wrong.

Your God is over there with all the prosperous people and the healthy people, the successful people, the popular and good-looking people, and you are over here alone in your trouble. Your God doesn't know any more about your trouble than the successful people know.

But as they thought about the crucified Jesus, they had to break out of that way of thinking. In Jesus' death God was saying to them, "For me to reveal myself, I not only have to take strength, process, growth, power, and health. I also have to take brokenness, weakness, disgrace, despair, and sorrow."

That was hard for the disciples to believe. But in the depth of their despair, the possibility occurred to them that Jesus' death might not have been God's curse, but his blessing. They went back and looked at the scriptures and suddenly they saw the suffering of God's chosen one showing up everywhere. When they talked to the Jews about Jesus as a crucified Lord, they had to be able to say, "Look, it's all there in the Bible," This was a tremendous turning point for them.

People who could never conceive of a crucified Messiah, began to see it first as a possibility, and then as a certainty. And that new certainty changed their picture of God and their picture of Jesus. They could never again think of God without including the suffering heart they saw revealed on the cross. When they saw Jesus and his cross as included in God, they saw God included in Jesus. They could never again think of Jesus without recognizing that God had been there all along. They had recognized Jesus as a great "prophet, mighty in deed and word before God and the people." Now they recognized him as "God with them." God was included in the meaning of Jesus. Jesus was included in the meaning of God.

However, opening up the scriptures to them was not enough. They still did not recognize him. Their eyes were opened when they shared the bread and the cup with him:

> By this time they had reached the village to which
> they were going, and he made as if to continue his

journey, but they pressed him: "Stay with us, for evening draws on, and the day is almost over." So he went in to stay with them. And when he had sat down with them at table, he took bread and said the blessing; he broke the bread, and offered it to them. Then their eyes were opened, and they recognized him; and he vanished from their sight. They said to one another, "Did we not feel our hearts on fire as he talked with us on the road and explained the scriptures to us?"

Without a moment's delay they set out and returned to Jerusalem. There they found that the Eleven and the rest of the company had assembled, and were saying, "It is true: the Lord has risen; he has appeared to Simon."

Then they gave their account of the events of their journey and told how he had been recognized by them at the breaking of the bread.

(Luke 24:28–35 NEB)

Their conflict about themselves and their hopes, and about the nature of God had been resolved. God appeared to them in a new light. Yet a new insight into scripture was not enough. They knew he was risen and was with them only when they participated together in a common meal, and he shared the loaf and cup he had asked them to share for the remembering of him. In the sharing of the bread and the cup, they knew he was alive and in their midst. God had restored the fact of Jesus. God had pronounced his Ultimate Yes over what had seemed a Final No.

The resurrection experience threw new light on Jesus' message and career. In that event, all the events of his career were transfigured. The disciples saw that God had been there all the time, and at no time more certainly than during his passion. The cross was God's new word about himself. He is our companion even through our death.

We do not read the story of the crucifixion as objective observers. We read it as those who know we are dealing with God, however hidden he may seem.

We read this story as members of a community that has found in it the clue to God's nature and purposes.

The disciples were empowered to face the No's of life because they had experienced the deepest Yes, when the crucified Messiah was present with them as their Living Lord. And so are we.

The disciples who had walked through the valley of death with him, discovered even there the power of life. And so have we.

The disciples discovered a constancy so much greater than their betrayals, that their failures faded into insignificance. And so have we.

We know about death. We are able to face it squarely — sustained by the power of his resurrection.

II

TO SHARE
HIS SUFFERING

> Almighty God, whose most dear Son went not up to
> joy but first he suffered pain, and entered not into
> glory before he was crucified: mercifully grant that
> we, walking in the way of the Cross, may find it none
> other than the way of life and peace; through Jesus
> Christ your Son our Lord.[1]

In parts II and III we will follow Jesus through his arrest, trial,
and crucifixion twice. The first time we will read the story as
told by Matthew and Mark and the second time by John. Matthew uses Mark's account and adds his own emphasis, particularly underscoring the way the events fulfill prophecies of
ancient writings. In the account of Matthew and Mark, Jesus
says less and less as the story reaches its climax, his only word
from the cross is the cry of abandonment, "My God, my God,
why hast thou forsaken me." He appears as the man of sorrow,
acquainted with grief. The story is a human tragedy of disappointed hopes. Hope for the success of Jesus' earthly mission is
lost, the faith and courage of his followers is lost, the humaneness of his enemies is eclipsed. We are face to face with a suffering Lord, whose suffering represents the suffering of all humankind. The story is a tragedy. In John's account, the scenes
are the same, but the lighting is different. For John the cross is a
triumph. The Johannine emphasis is described in the Introduction to Part III, "Reigning from the Tree."

7

Is It I, Lord?

And when it was evening he came with the twelve. And as they were at table eating, Jesus said, "Truly, I say to you, one of you will betray me, one who is eating with me." They began to be sorrowful, and to say to him one after another, "Is it I?" He said to them, "It is one of the twelve, one who is dipping bread in the same dish with me. For the Son of man goes as it is written of him, but woe to that man by whom the Son of man is betrayed! It would have been better for that man if he had not been born."

And as they were eating, he took bread, and blessed, and broke it, and gave it to them, and said, "Take; this is my body." And he took a cup, and when he had given thanks he gave it to them, and they all drank of it. And he said to them, "This is my blood of the covenant, which is poured out for many. Truly, I say to you, I shall not drink again of the fruit of the vine until that day when I drink it new in the kingdom of God."

And when they had sung a hymn, they went out to the Mount of Olives. And Jesus said to them, "You will all fall away; for it is written, 'I will strike the shepherd, and the sheep will be scattered.' But after I am raised up, I will go before you to Galilee." Peter said to him, "Even though they all fall away, I will not." And Jesus said to him, "Truly, I say to you, this very night, before the cock crows twice, you will deny me three times." But he said vehemently, "If I must die with you, I will not deny you." And they all said the same.

(Mark 14:17-31 RSV)

Lord, is it I?

I don't like that question, Lord.

Why do you always ask it?

O.K. you don't ask it. I ask it.

But I always seem to ask it when I am with you.

I don't like asking, "Is it I?"

I want to feel good about myself, Lord.

I don't want always to take the blame.

Of course I make mistakes. Everybody does, but I do the best I can.

Nobody's perfect.

I don't do well when I feel bad about myself, Lord.

You know that.

When I feel guilty I get angry or I get depressed.

Either way, I don't do well.

I have to feel right about myself.

It is important for me to know I'm O.K.

All my life people have been making me feel bad about myself.

> It's your fault.
>
> You were bad.
>
> Don't touch that, it's dirty.
>
> Don't treat your brothers that way, it's not nice.
>
> Don't lie to me.
>
> What did you do to her?
>
> How could you be so awful?

I'm tired of all that, Lord.

I want to be stroked. I want some warm feelings.

> I'm tired of that question, "Is it I?"
>
> I can't stand it anymore.

I am either right or I'm wrong.

I am capable and adequate, and kind, a person of integrity, or I am nothing.

If I can't feel strong, I am going to feel helpless.

If I can't always win, I'm a loser.

If I feel mean and small, I am going to be mean and small.

So look at me and tell me that I'm O.K., I'm good, I'm right.
Don't keep asking me, "Is it you?"

It's not my fault.

If I don't always measure up, it's because of the kind of family I had.

I never got enough love, Lord. How can you expect me to give it away?

I am a little demanding of other people, but other people make lots of demands on me.

I have to look out for myself, that's the way things are.

Good guys finish last, Lord.

You have to cut it a little close here and there.

If you have to play up to people who can help you, you do.

If you have to bribe, you do.

That's the way the system works, Lord. I didn't invent it.

I just have to survive in it.

If he or she were more considerate of my needs,

If he or she showed more appreciation of me.

If he or she really enjoyed me, loved me, cared for me,

Then . . . I'd be better.

No Lord, it's not me, it's them.

Why don't you ask them that question?

What did you do Lord, when you knew your friends would betray you? What did you say when they asked you, "Is it I?"

You said it would be very hard for them.

Their betrayal would make them sorry they were born.

I don't want to feel like that, Lord.

I want you to get off my case.

I want you to comfort me, hold me, tell me I'm all right.

Feed me.

That's what you did to them.

Knowing they would betray you, you fed them.

Take eat, you said.

Take drink, you said.

The food and drink you gave them, you said would wash away all their failures.

That bread and wine was to strengthen them so they could return and take up your cause again.

You fed them. You comforted them.

You told them they would have to take responsibility for what they did, whatever it was, but that their betrayal was not the end.

You never expected them to be perfect, did you, Lord.

They didn't have to be righteous for you to care for them.

You didn't expect them to be as strong as they believed they were.

You knew them.

You know me, too, Lord. You know how I am.

You share your life with me knowing all that I have done and will do.

Being strong and righteous and adequate is not the price of admission to your table.

If I really believed that, Lord. If I knew it in my bones, then your question wouldn't bother me.

If I experienced your love, Lord, perhaps I could admit it.

Yes, I have done those things I ought not to have done.

Perhaps I could take responsibility for those things.

Perhaps I could take it on myself and stop putting it on my mother, my mate, my boss or the system.

Putting it on them is what makes me weak.

I am strong enough to take it on myself.

I do not have to shrink from that question, "Is it I?"

Yes, of couse, it is, Lord. It is I.

8

Abba, Father . . .
Take This Cup Away from Me

When they reached a place called Gethsemane, he said to his disciples, "Sit here while I pray." And he took Peter and James and John with him. Horror and dismay came over him, and he said to them, "My heart is ready to break with grief; stop here, and stay awake." Then he went forward a little, threw himself on the ground, and prayed that, if it were possible, this hour might pass him by. "Abba, Father," he said, "all things are possible to thee; take this cup away from me. Yet not what I will, but what thou wilt."

He came back and found them asleep; and he said to Peter, "Asleep, Simon? Were you not able to stay awake for one hour? Stay awake, all of you; and pray that you may be spared the test. The spirit is willing, but the flesh is weak."

Once more he went away and prayed.

On his return he found them asleep again, for their eyes were heavy; and they did not know how to answer him. The third time he came and said to them, "Still sleeping? Still taking your ease? Enough! The hour has come. The son of man is betrayed to sinful men. Up, let us go forward! My betrayer is upon us."

(Mark 14:32–42 NEB)

It seemed to be all over.
You had said goodbye to your friends.
You had not tried to stop your betrayer.
It was only a matter of time.
But you could still run away.
Perhaps the inevitable could be averted.
God, your Father might stay the hand of your enemies.
After all, everything and anything is possible for God.
And you were special to him.
You called him "Abba"
That was more like "Daddy" than Father.
You talked to him like a little child,
    dependent on his parent,
    confident of his parents' care.
A little child has the right to make demands on his daddy.
A daddy is supposed to take care of the infant.
You had a claim on his attention and concern.
You had a right to turn from the source of your life,
    the one who had called you to his place,
    and ask for help.
You really believed all things were possible.
You prayed with expectation.
You didn't assume the system was closed.
You could escape. You could fight. He could save you.
    I don't pray like that Lord.
    I don't expect a great deal.
    I assume that everything is determined by circumstances
    over which I have no control.
    I can't change. I am caught in the same old patterns that
    haven't worked before.
The people who are hassling me won't change.
The cancer cells are growing beyond anyone's power to stop
them.
It almost seems useless to pray.
Or when I pray I hedge my bets by saying,

"If it is thy will, heal this person.

but if not, help her to accept the inevitable."

You don't start out by praying for strength to accept the inevitable. You know what you want—your life, and you do not hesitate to ask for it. You start to pray assuming all things are possible. Yours is an open universe.

God is alive. He can act . . . if he wants to.

Take it away from me.

Let me out of this.

Don't make me go through it.

Turn this inevitable tragedy into something else.

Three times you asked.

You wrestled with God for a favorable verdict.

You sweat blood over it.

I have heard this story so often, Lord, that I rush too quickly to the punch line—"Not what I will, but what thou wilt."

You do not assume that because you want something very much it can't be God's will.

When I was a little boy, people read stories to me from a book called *Inspired Children*. It was full of edifying accounts of youngsters who talked to God and looked for his guidance. In one of those stories a child said he received guidance from God to sit in the rumble seat on a class trip. The teacher doubted if this was really the voice of God and said, "If the message was that Johnny, and Billy, and Bobby were to sit in the rumble seat and you in the front seat, that would have been God speaking. But God does not usually tell you you can have what you want when everyone else wants the same thing."

That story made a strong impression on me, Lord.

It told me that God's will is usually opposed to what I want.

If something was pleasurable and attractive, God can't mean me to have it.

You did not assume that.

You were not afraid or ashamed to ask for what you wanted.

Your prayer expressed the deepest longing of your heart. Prayer was a way to get clear about your hopes, and to press God, who *could* do anything, for their fulfillment.

You asked again and again and again.

But in the end you did not have your way.

In the end you accepted.

God does not yield easily, even to you.

But why go through all the sweat and agony of wrestling with him if he's going to do what he's going to do?

I guess when you wrestle with God you have to be willing to put your whole life at stake.

I can't ask God to become involved in my life and then withhold something of myself — what I really want.

When I am too prudent and careful in my praying, my prayers become unreal, even to me. Only by taking him, and what I really want, seriously can my prayers make any difference.

To be sure, in the end, I have to accept my limits.

But I too quickly turn the responsibility over to God with a "whatever you say."

That cuts me off from the relationship with him.

The young boy who grudgingly submits to a father he knows is going to have his way in the end, who refuses to struggle for the shape of his own life with the powers that control his destiny, will never discover what is possible.

And he will never understand his father.

"If it is God's will" is what we say when we reach the limit beyond which we cannot push.

But acquiescence is not a simple thing. We can not love the one who limits us without a struggle.

We must care, and not care.

Only in the struggle with the one who imposes limits upon us will we come to know Him and know ourselves as well.

Only after we say what we really want, and struggle to wrest it from God's hands, even after our friends have turned their eyes away from us and escaped into anxious sleep, only *then* will we be able to love the One who walks beside us whom we will know very well.

9

They All Deserted Him and Ran Away

While he was still speaking, Judas, one of the Twelve, appeared; with him a great crowd armed with swords and cudgels, sent by the chief priests and the elders of the nation. The traitor gave them this sign: "The one I kiss is your man; seize him"; and stepping forward at once, he said, "Hail Rabbi!" and kissed him. Jesus replied, "Friend, do what you are here to do." They then came forward, seized Jesus, and held him fast.

At that moment one of those with Jesus reached for his sword and drew it out, and he struck at the High Priest's servant and cut off his ear. But Jesus said to him, "Put up your sword. All who take the sword die by the sword. . . ." Then the disciples all deserted him and ran away.

(Matthew 26:47-52, 56b NEB)

They all ran out on you, Jesus.
They scattered among the shadows of the olive trees.
They hid themselves in the bushes.
They kept going until they were out of sight, out of sound,
   out of breath.
Get away.
Break free.
Don't get involved in this.

It is all coming to a bad end.

Hide. Save yourself. Life is precious.

For reasons of your own
>   you were determined to die.

But it wasn't fair to ask them to follow you that far.

In Galilee it was different.
>   You were warm-hearted and festive.

>   You were popular.

>   You healed the sick

>   You inspired them by your teaching.

>   You were kind and helpful.

>   You challenged the old ways and the new rulers.

>   You were exciting.

>   You were so close to God, so sure the new age was about
to dawn.

>   You were optimistic and a joy to be around.

But you have changed.

You started to talk about death all the time.

They couldn't handle that, Jesus.

Suffering and death they hadn't bargained for.

They couldn't follow you on that road.

So while you struggled, they fell asleep.

They had to. How much could they take?

When Judas came with the soldiers, they knew it was all over.

They had two choices: to fight or to take flight.
>   You made them put up the sword, there was nothing left
but flight.

>   You wouldn't let them fight, so they had to run.

I understand them, Jesus.

There is no point in sticking to a hopeless cause.

I run away too.

Physical death doesn't often threaten me.

But I run away from trouble.

I don't like conflict.

I shrink from pain, physical pain and psychic pain.

Why should I let myself get involved with pain and death?

Hostile people frighten me, I want to keep out of their way.
Dirty, sick, troubled people upset me.
    Why do I have to go near them?
I can't afford to get sucked into other people's problems.
They overwhelm me. I have to keep my distance.
Sometimes I have to take off.

I want to be faithful.
    I want to be helpful.
But there comes a time when I have to say,
    "Thus far, and no farther."
    Enough. Cut your losses. Let it go.
    Walk away from it.
    There is nothing more I can do!
That's the way it's got to be Lord. You understand that, don't you?
    Why do you ask me to be present while you suffer?
    Why do you ask me to be present with others who suffer?
    Why do you ask me to be present to my own suffering?
I watched my mother die with cancer, Lord.
It was not a pretty sight.
I did not want to talk to her about it.
We all went to see her, but then we wanted to get away quickly.
We pretended it wasn't happening.
We kept telling her how well she looked and how she would get better.
    We knew she wouldn't and she knew she wouldn't.
So she had to face it alone — the most important experience of her life — because none of us could face it with her.
Even the doctor didn't want to be around much.
It seemed better that way.
Less pain all around.
But she didn't die quickly. We got impatient with her for holding on so long. We were impatient because the most important thing we couldn't talk about. When it was too late to talk about it, we were ashamed.

We all forsook her and fled.
We thought we were fleeing from death.
Actually, we were running from life.

I need to run away from death, Lord.
You understand that, don't you?
You know I will return again.
  but just for a little while, let me protect myself.
  I'll come back, but I have to run now, Lord.
Even if running away from death means running away from
life.
I've got to run, Lord.
Unless you hold me.
Unless you help me stop running.
Unless you help me stay with the pain and the dirt, the conflict
and the confusion.
Unless you help me bear my losses.
When I run Lord, go with me. Come after me.
Don't let me go. I want to run.
Maybe I can stay. Hold me, Lord.

10

He Went Out and
Wept Bitterly

Meanwhile Peter was sitting outside in the courtyard when a serving maid accosted him and said, "You were there too with Jesus the Galilean." Peter denied it in face of them all. "I do not know what you mean," he said.

He then went out to the gateway, where another girl, seeing him, said to the people there, "This fellow was with Jesus of Nazareth." Once again he denied it, saying with an oath, "I do not know the man."

Shortly afterwards the bystanders came up and said to Peter, "Surely you are one of them; your accent gives you away!" At this he broke into curses and declared with an oath: "I do not know this man."

At that moment a cock crew; and Peter remembered how Jesus had said, "Before the cock crows you will disown me three times." He went outside, and wept bitterly.

(Matthew 26:69–75 NEB)

Peter was the strong one.

He was always taking charge.

He was the most insightful student of his rabbi.

He was physically vigorous and fearless —

the kind of man psychologists would describe as having great ego strength.

He had promised Jesus just a few hours ago that though every-

one else would fail him, Peter would stick to the end.
He had run away with all the rest, but he had come back.
He entered the place of the trial
      watching to see how it all turned out.
That took a lot of guts.
But when someone remembered having seen him with Jesus, he
played dumb.
"I do not know what you mean."
He didn't owe them an honest answer. He was under no obliga-
tion to tell the truth to the enemy.
But they were not put off.
      "You have a northern accent. Jesus is from the north.
      Are you sure you are not one of them?"
In a burst of anger he curses, "I do not know the man!"
The cock crows and Peter remembers Jesus' words:
      "Before the cock crows you will deny me three times."
And he went out and wept bitterly.
I wonder what Peter was weeping about.
It was not for you that he wept.
Your situation was no better or worse.
You were going to die.
Peter had come to see the end.
Why the bitter tears?
The bitter tears were for Peter.
The bitter tears were for the death of the old Peter.
      Peter the strong
      Peter the true
      Peter the man in charge
His tears were for the death of Peter in control;
      Peter on top of things
      Peter the man of integrity
      Peter the faithful friend
      Peter the afraid-of-nobody
      Peter the superior to his weak brothers
These were all self images very dear to Peter.
He had depended on them for the meaning of his life.

Those were the things that made him special, different, admir-
able.
In one moment of clarity
 he saw they were not the real Peter
The real Peter was the one who to protect himself
 would deny with a curse even knowing a friend he
 had sworn to stand by to the death.
His tears were tears of mourning for his lost self-esteem.
It was a terrible loss.
He wept bitterly.

In charge. On top of things. Integrity. Courage.
I try to be like that, Lord.
Most of the time I'm pretty good at it.
I bear my share around the house, around the office.
I work very hard. People depend on me.
Sometimes I'm tough, but I am reasonable.
I get a lot done.
Sometimes I have bad luck, or I take a job too big for me, and
things don't work out the way I like.
But I'm a fair man, I don't ask anyone to do something I wouldn't
do myself.
That's the way I am. Or that's the way I thought I was.
Last week my secretary quit because she said, I was thoughtless
and unreasonable.
She was a good secretary. I didn't want to lose her.
I don't know what happened.
I thought she knew I appreciated her.
 I gave her raises when I could. I took her out to lunch now
and then.
I know I criticized her work sometimes, and even lost my temper
 with her, but that's part of the job.
 My work gets criticized — more often and less fairly.
She said I was a sexist.
 that I didn't respect her as a person
 or treat her as an equal.

I couldn't believe it. I thought she must be getting her period.
When I got home, I got no sympathy from my wife.
She said my secretary was right and launched into a
diatribe about how thoughtless I was at home,
 how neglectful of her and the children,
 how bossy and authoritarian I had become.
She went on and on, and as she talked everything I believed
about myself began to come apart: the kind of man I was, the
kind of father I was, the kind of employer I was — it was all erod-
ed by the acid of her tongue.
Suddenly I knew that deep down somewhere in this woman I
loved there was a pool of hurt and anger I had never glimpsed.
I had hurt her.
But I didn't understand how I had done it.
Or how I could be different.
I began to cry.
She began to cry.
I reached out to her. She held me. I held her.
We really do love each other.
But where do we go from here?
Is there a life for us beyond this death?

I see you speaking to Peter beside another charcoal fire.
I see you speaking to him by the sea where he earned his living.
I see you coming back to him when he thought you were gone,
asking him one question, over and over, as if it were all that
mattered.

Do you love me? Feed my sheep.
Do you love me? Feed my sheep.
Do you love me? Feed my sheep.

You offered him a new life in place of the old Peter who had
died.

I am waiting Lord. Come by me, Lord.

11

I Have Betrayed
Innocent Blood

When Judas the traitor saw that Jesus had been condemned, he was seized with remorse, and returned the thirty silver pieces to the chief priests and elders.

"I have sinned," he said; "I have brought an innocent man to his death." But they said, "What is that to us? See to that yourself." So he threw the money down in the temple and left them, and went and hanged himself.

(Matthew 27:3-5 NEB)

We don't know why Judas betrayed you, Lord.
The gospels don't give us any clues.
It certainly wasn't for money.
Of the different motives that have been ascribed to him in Christian history, one has as much historical basis as the other.
We just don't know why he did it.
But the fact remains. It just stands there. He was a traitor.
The gospels focus on Judas' reaction, not his motivation.
When he saw what he had done, he repented.
He tried to undo the damage.
He went to the priests and confessed that he was wrong.
He tried to give back the money.
The priests and elders would not help him undo his wrong.

They refused to take the money.
They refused to stop the process he had started.
His guilt was of no importance to them.
That was his problem.
>"What is that to us?" they asked.
>"See to it yourself."

Judas saw only two choices before him: innocence or death.
He tried to become innocent again, but he could not.
>"All the king's horses, and all the king's men,
>couldn't put humpty-dumpty together again."

It was too late. Jesus' death was now certain and Judas was responsible.
He could not go on living as a guilty man.
If innocence was impossible, the alternative was to end his life.
He had to act. He could not wait. It was too late.
Peter too had betrayed his Lord.
Peter too had come face to face with himself as a guilty man.
Peter's repentance led to tears and to waiting.
What would have happened, Lord, if Judas had not tried to "see to it" himself?
What would have happened if he had waited?
>If he had faced himself in your presence.

Would you have held out your hand to him?
He couldn't do it for himself.
Would you have done it for him?

I know what it is to hurt innocent people, Lord.
I have done things of which I am deeply ashamed.
There are memories I have to bury because I cannot face them.
I knew I shouldn't have driven the car that evening.
After work I went to a bar for a drink which turned into two or three.
I should not have tried to drive home.
The little girl dashed out between the parked cars and into the traffic.

When I saw her, it was too late.
My reactions were too slow.
I felt the hard steel of the car strike her soft body.
The ambulance, the police, the hospital, the stricken parents
. . . I saw them all through a haze.
I could not bear to see the parents.
I did not want to look at my wife and children.
I did not want to look at myself in the mirror.
When I heard she would be crippled for life, I wanted to die.
I couldn't live with what I had done.

But I didn't die.
The parents didn't want me to see the child.
They didn't want to talk to me except through their lawyers.
I didn't blame them.
I finally sneaked into the hospital room. I don't know why I had
to go or where I got the courage.
The child lay there. Her legs, which would never run again, lay
lifeless beneath the sheets.
She recognized me.
I stood by her bed, tears running down my cheeks.
She took my hand and lifted it to her mouth and kissed it.

There was nothing I could do.
The only one who could help me was that broken child.
From somewhere deep within her heart, deep within your heart,
Lord, she "saw to" my guilt.
She gave me back my life.

I know what it is to betray innocent blood.
I have done things I can't undo.
I have learned there are times when there is nothing to do, but
be still
      and wait —
Wait for you to find a way to overcome

my evil with your good,
my hate with your love,
my death dealing with your life giving.
Only you can see to it, Lord. I cannot see to it.
I have betrayed innocent blood.

I will arise and go to my father and I will say to him,
"Father, I have sinned against heaven and before you,
    and am no more worthy to be called your son."

I will be still and wait for the word.

"Go in peace, the Lord has put away your sins."

✳ 12

My Hands Are Clean

Jesus was now brought before the Governor; and as he stood there the Governor asked him, "Are you the King of the Jews?"

"The words are yours," said Jesus; and to the charges laid against him by the chief priests and elders he made no reply. Then Pilate said to him, "Do you not hear all this evidence that is brought against you?"; but he still refused to answer one word, to the Governor's great astonishment. . . .

At the festival season it was the Governor's custom to release one prisoner chosen by the people. There was then in custody a man of some notoriety, called Jesus Bar-Abbas. When they were assembled Pilate said to them, "Which would you like me to re-lease to you—Jesus Bar-Abbas, or Jesus called Messiah?" For he knew that it was out of malice that they had brought Jesus be-fore him. . . . While Pilate was sitting in court a message came to him from his wife; "Have nothing to do with that innocent man; I was much troubled on his account in my dreams last night."

Meanwhile the chief priests and elders had persuaded the crowd to ask for the release of Bar-Abbas and to have Jesus put to death. So when the Governor asked, " Which of the two do you wish me to release to you?" they said, "Bar-Abbas." "Then what am I to do with Jesus called Messiah?" asked Pilate: and with one voice they answered, "Crucify him!" "Why, what harm has he done?" Pilate asked; but they shouted all the louder,

"Crucify him!" Pilate could see that nothing was being gained, and a riot was starting; so he took water and washed his hands in full view of the people, saying "My hands are clean of this man's blood; see to that yourselves."

(Matthew 27:11-26 NEB)

Poor Pilate. He was damned if he did and damned if he didn't. He was just trying to do his job.

He had come up to Jerusalem for this Passover holiday to keep order.

He knew these people he had to rule over were a little crazy. They regularly got carried away by fantasies of glory. Actually, they were a pitiful race of ragamuffins. They certainly were not Romans, that's for sure. You couldn't reason with them as sensible people.

Palestine was not an easy post. The climate was terrible. His wife hated the life here. It was one of those jobs you had to do if you wanted to get ahead in the civil service, but it was full of pitfalls. It could blow up and end his career.

These crazy people never gave up.

They kept making hopeless gestures of revolt which had to be put down — often bloodily.

And they were never more truculent than at the time of their Passover Festival. Passover kept alive the memory of the time they said their tribal God had freed them from the Egyptians. It was quite important in such an unsettled time for Pilate to be strong.

The Jews had to be reminded that the Roman Emperor was no hapless Pharoah.

The trick was to be firm with them without provoking any ugly incident.

The man standing before him had created quite a ruckus the previous Sunday with his "spontaneous" parade into town on that donkey with everyone shouting about the "son of David" coming to claim his city.

It was all nonsense of course, but given the crowds and the excitement, it could have got out of hand.

The way you went into the temple and turned over the tables of the businessmen was unsettling, if slightly amusing from the Roman point of view.

Fussing about the temple was harmless enough, but you could never tell when your direct action would lead to a serious disturbance of the peace.

And peace was what Pilate was there to protect.

Why couldn't these Jews accept the Roman peace?

Goodness knows they had a lot of freedom.

They were allowed to continue to worship their strange God.

The taxes were heavy to be sure, but they got a reasonable return in government services.

If everyone would just accept the realities and go about his own business, there would be peace.

But these people had this crazy streak in them that led them to throw themselves against the Roman spears, senselessly. Now here they were again, bringing him this Jesus. They didn't have the courtesy to come into his house. That would defile them, the stiff neck bastards! He already had three real crooks to crucify. That was enough to demonstrate he was still in charge. They apparently wanted to add this temple reformer to his list, otherwise they would have punished him themselves.

He didn't see why he should go along with them.

He didn't like taking a man's life for no reason.

But he had to listen. With luck it wouldn't take too long.

There was a lot to attend to this week.

When he sees that his efforts to talk sense to them, do not avail and that he is going to have a riot on his hands, not to mention an angry wife, he decides he doesn't want to take the responsibility. This is one man's blood that won't be on his hands. He will let them do what they want to do, but he will wash his hands of the whole affair. He doesn't want the responsibility of choice.

Let them do what they want, but don't blame him.
His hands will be clean of this man's blood.

It is hard to keep clean in this life, Lord.
It is hard to take responsibility for our actions.
Sometimes we think that if we don't act, the problem will go
away.
But it is hard not to act, too.
Demands for decision come from every side.
If we act, we get in trouble.
If we don't act, we get in trouble.
We are damned if we do and damned if we don't.
We try not to make a decision.
But we know that not to decide is to decide.

There is someone I ought to fire, Lord.
She is undermining her co-workers.
She isn't doing the job.
She is too angry to take help.
Firing her will only make her more angry.
She will drag me through the procedure.
She will claim she is being discriminated against because she is a
woman.
There will be hearings and paperwork.
It will be a mess, Lord.
I'd like to take it to my boss, and get him to do it.
Or transfer her to another department and let them handle it.
I don't want to be the bad guy. Why do I have to decide?

My son keeps doing things that are getting him into trouble.
If I am consistently stern about it, and punish him and try to
help him learn, he may become so resentful that I will lose all
communication with him.
If I don't try to stop him, if I ignore it and let it go, what will
happen to him?
"He who is soft when he should be hard will be cruel when he

should be kind" — I read that somewhere.
I'm damned if I do and damned if I don't.
Why do I have to decide? I only want peace.
Is that too much to ask?

People are always asking me to take sides — to do something.
I am always getting caught between those who say "no don't,"
like my wife, and those who say, "but you have to," like my
friends who are worked up about an issue.
They kept telling me I should put my body on the line to stop the
killing in Vietnam.
But I didn't know enough about it, Lord.
Who could I believe?
How could I decide?
I voted for the President because he said, everybody said, he was
a man of peace.
When he said the war was necessary, he certainly knew more
than I did.
How could I take that responsibility on myself?
It wasn't up to me. It was very complicated.
Now they are telling me that to keep peace in the world, to stop
inflation, our government must stop spending money on the
needs of people, and give it to the military.
Other people are asking me to protest again.
I know the government is too big, too powerful, too intrusive.
The old ways weren't working. Inflation is killing all of us.
Something had to be done.
The people elected a man who says he knows the way to go.
It's his responsibility.
I don't have a better plan.
Let them see to it, it might work.
Anyway, it's not my responsibility.
Nobody can take responsibility for all the problems of the
world.
I can't set myself up as judge of the universe.
I am not you, Christ.

I do not have to redeem the world by my action and my suffering,
I can only know so much, I can only care so much,
The issues are very complicated.

Do I have to choose?
Do I have to know?
Do I have to care?

Why me, Lord.
Why you, Lord?
Why did you stretch out your arms upon the cross offering your life for the whole world?
You don't expect me to do that, do you?

13

They Beat Him

Pilate's soldiers then took Jesus into the Governor's headquarters, where they collected the whole company round him. They stripped him and dressed him in a scarlet mantle; and plaiting a crown of thorns they placed it on his head, with a cane in his right hand. Falling on their knees before him they jeered at him: "Hail, King of the Jews!"

They spat on him, and used the cane to beat him about the head. When they had finished their mockery, they took off the mantle and dressed him in his own clothes.

Then they led him away to be crucified.

On their way they met a man from Cyrene, Simon by name, and pressed him into service to carry his cross. So they came to a place called Golgotha (which means "Place of a skull") and there he was offered a draught of wine mixed with gall; but when he had tasted it he would not drink.

After fastening him to the cross they divided his clothes among them by casting lots, and then sat down there to keep watch. Over his head was placed the inscription giving the charge: "This is Jesus, the king of the Jews."

Two bandits were crucified with him, one on his right and the other on his left.

(Matthew 27:27-38 NEB)

They enjoyed doing it to you, Lord, didn't they.

They enjoyed taking you down.

Somehow you threatened them.

Powerless, you had the power to make them feel weak and help-less.

You, the simple Galilean prophet were a threat to them,
    their power system
    their way of life,
    the rightness of their moral code.

You challenged everything they believed, wanted, felt.

You so enraged them that they decided to show you how one who pretended to be a King over them would be treated.

They made a crown of thorns and pressed it into your head until the blood ran down your cheeks.

They put a purple robe on you and mocked you with false obeisance.

After that there were the nails driven with heavy mallets through soft flesh into hard boards.

Horrible, but fascinating.

They would show you. Your blood touched a lust for punishment in them.

They had the power to take your life.

A life was being snuffed out and they were doing it.

They were alive and you were dying.

They were no longer powerless. They were killers.

How could they do it?

How could they take such pleasure in inflicting pain?

I know how they could, Lord.

Once I left my car in a parking garage overnight.

Five dollars up to twelve hours, the sign said.

When I came back after ten hours, the attendant asked for nine dollars.

He was extorting four dollars out of me.

Only four dollars, but I was enraged.

I felt powerless and impotent.

I was so crazy with anger that I would willingly have nailed him to the wall.

I would have hit him, battered him, crucified him — gladly.

Nothing would have been too bad for him.

I did not know myself.

I am a peaceful man. But some button had been touched.

For four dollars I was ready to be a killer?

Yes, it is in me, too, Lord.

I have led a protected life. I have suffered little unfairness.

What must it be like for all those who all their lives have been humiliated, pushed around, robbed of dignity.

It is not so hard to understand the rage and fire and destruction which breaks out among the deprived.

There are times when evil is so monstrous, when violence is committed on a people for so long, that there is nothing to be done but to accept powerlessness, or show power with violence.

The murder of the Jews by the Nazis had to be punished with counter violence.

When the exploited and the poor are finally so enraged that they burst out against the powers that hold them down, someone gets hurt.

Every revolution and counter revolution is bloody.

Injustice always involves suffering.

It is either the suffering of those who accept the injustice, or the injustice they impose or is imposed on them when they fight back.

Where there is injustice, there is a cross.

Someone always gets killed.

Is there no way to justice without violence?

Your love was so powerful Lord, they felt helpless before it.

In rage and anger they did what hate always does with love, they crucified you.

History is dotted with such crosses.

It continues.

Crowns of thorns are still pushed into soft flesh.

Nails are still hammered into upturned palms.

Electric shocks are applied to genitals.
Persons are still reduced to things.
The PLO attacks the Israelis and the Israelis, for centuries the
suffering ones, attack the PLO.
And the cycle goes on and on.
Is there no way to break it, Lord?
Is there no way to keep from falling into blood lust when we are
threatened?
There are teenagers on our street, Lord.
They frighten us.
They sit on our stoops and throw things in our windows.
They are violent ones.
They challenge us.
They enrage us.
Call the police.
Get them out of here.
They have no homes, no jobs, no hopes.
No matter what you have to do, get them off the street.
    Get them out of sight.
We will not have our lives disturbed by their noises.
We do not want to watch their self-destruction.
Lock them up.
Beat them up.
Do anything, but get rid of them.

It's there, Lord.
It's in me.
It's there in our neighborhood.
It's there in our country.
It's there in Africa, in Ireland, in the Holy Land.
When will it end, Lord?
Will there always be crosses?
You said, "Those who take the sword will perish by the sword."
But Lord, sword is in all of us.
Is death in all of us too?

14

They Hurled Abuse at Him

The passers-by hurled abuse at him: they wagged their heads
and cried, "You would pull the temple down, would you, and
build it in three days? Come down from the cross and save yourself, if you are indeed the Son of God." So too the chief priest
with the lawyers and elders mocked at him: "He saved others,"
they said, "but he cannot save himself. King of Israel, indeed!
Let him come down now from the cross, and then we will believe
him. Did he trust in God? Let God rescue him, if he wants
him — for he said he was God's Son." Even the bandits who were
crucified with him taunted him in the same way.

(Matthew 27:39-44 NEB)

You hung there, Jesus, in the heat of the day.
Flies and gnats buzzing around the blood that pulsed from your
wounds.
Stripped naked, with no control over bladder or bowels, you
were a disgusting sight.
    "[He has] . . . no beauty that we should desire him.
    He was despised and rejected by men. . . .
    As one from whom men hide their faces
    He was despised, and we esteemed him not."

(Isaiah 53:2-3)

The sight of you did not draw forth pity, or outrage at injustice.
Instead it brought forth derision, mockery, taunts, and cruelty.

Instead of wondering why you were there, they assumed you
brought it on yourself by your pretension.

No one could act the way you acted and talk the way you talked
and expect to get away with it.

It was your own fault.

Nobody gave you the right to challenge the law of Moses,
>the authority of the priests
>the practices of the temple
>the power of Caesar's representative.

The Son of God, indeed.

If you were God's son, surely God would help you.

Where is he now?

Where are the angels that would bear you up lest you stub your
foot against a stone?

That such a dirty, smelly, bleeding man would make such
claims, was an outrage.

Even the bandits were offended.

There seems to be something in the human animal that hates a
loser,
>that turns on the one that stumbles,
>that picks the last feather out of the hurt chicken.

You were a loser Jesus, and it was your own fault.

It is always the loser's fault isn't it?
>The woman who is raped must have been asking for it.
>The Jews in Germany must have brought on the Holocaust.
>The poor in the crowded cities prey on each other and cut
each other up, because that's the kind of people they are.
>They bring it on themselves.
>What do you expect?

The sight of suffering moves us as quickly to cruelty as to pity.

We have to be converted to sympathy.
>It is our nature to hate the ugly, the helpless, the injured.

Yesterday, Lord, a helpless wreck of a man asked me for food.
>He was dirty.
>He was limping.

His eyes were glazed.

He insisted on my attention.

"I am hungry," he said. "Give me something to eat."

I looked at him and felt my heart turn against him.

I did not want to help him.

I thought I should help him.

He had no right to insist on what was mine.

He had no right to intrude into my busy life.

I felt obligated to help him.

I didn't want to associate with him.

I knew that if I gave him something he would go away and my discomfort would go away.

The simplest way was to give him what he wanted.

But what right did he have to make me feel uncomfortable?

I was angry that he could do that.

Deep in my heart I would like to have struck him.

I would like to have driven his disconcerting features out of my life.

I wanted to hurt him, Lord. I didn't want to help him.

Why was that, Lord? Why did his claim on my charity make me so angry?

And so afraid? Because I was afraid.

I was afraid of the anger in my heart.

I was afraid of his anger toward me whom he saw as prosperous, well fed, secure.

But I did not feel secure.

He reminded me that I too am hungry,

 and helpless

 and dependent upon the kindness of strangers.

I did not like that, Lord.

I wanted to get rid of that.

I wanted to put a gulf between us.

 to make it clear to him, and to me,

 that we were not alike.

It is his own fault that he is in that state.

I might have given up and gone that way . . .

But I didn't.
Why couldn't he be like me?
I would never get myself in that situation.
I am stronger, and wiser, and better than that.
We are not alike.
He is not human.
He has no right to ask me to care for him.
I am not responsible for him,
I have trouble enough taking care of myself.
Get off my back. Get out of my sight.
I am not responsible for you.

I have to assume that people get what they deserve.
If I began to think otherwise,
    then the unpleasant creature is innocent
    and the government and the priests and all the
    good people are wrong, and the whole system is wrong.
That can't be.
We can't have a world in which there is no justice.
We can't have a world where the evil prosper and the innocent
get crucified.
We can't have a world where the sun and the rain fall equally on
the just and the unjust.
That would be an ugly world.
    a world without meaning
    an evil world.
So he has to be wrong.
It must be his fault.
He is stupid, he is no good. He deserves it.
    But then, there you are on the cross.
    The most innocent, the best, the most deserving.
    And here we are mocking you, despising you,
    counting you among the refuse of the world.
    And you stretch out your arms on the cross,
    and embrace the whole world with your love.

Jesus, how can I break out of the circle of fear and anger and guilt that makes me strike out at the victim?

Help me to accept the neediness, the helplessness, the dependency in myself, so that I will not have to punish it in other people. Help me to see the victims of the world
>as brothers and sisters,
>of yours, and of mine.

What will it take to melt my heart, Lord, if your cross doesn't do it?

15

Lord Have Mercy

A number of women were also present, watching from a distance; they had followed Jesus from Galilee and waited on him. Among them were Mary of Magdala, Mary the mother of James and Joseph, and the mother of the sons of Zebedee. When evening fell, there came a man of Arimathaea, Joseph by name, who was a man of means, and had himself become a disciple of Jesus. He approached Pilate, and asked for the body of Jesus; and Pilate gave orders that he should have it.

Joseph took the body, wrapped it in a clean linen sheet, and laid it in his own unused tomb, which he had cut out of the rock; he then rolled a large stone against the entrance, and went away. Mary of Magdala was there and the other Mary, sitting opposite the grave.

(Matthew 27:55-61 NEB)

Well, it is all over Lord.
And yet it is not all over.
We have watched you die, once again.
We have looked once again at your dying all around us.
We have looked at the dying of the poor.
We have looked at the dying of our self-esteem.
We have looked at our betrayals.
We have looked at our irresponsibility.
We have looked at our rage.

You are dead now.
You are lying peacefully in your mother's arms.
You are lying in the tomb of a friend.
You are sealed in the sepulcher.
They have made it as secure as they can.

Somehow in the face of your death and our death,
    our betrayals and our fear
    and our angers and our irresponsibility
don't seem to matter so much.
They are there and they will be there.
They separate us from each other and from you.
We should care and not care about them.
In the face of the mystery of your life and death they become un-
important.
It is not that having looked at them,
    we will go our way and sin no more.
It is not that having looked at them,
    by some giant effort of our will,
    we will be different.

But perhaps, Lord, having seen them all again
    we will glimpse our common humanity.
For we are all together in our weakness.
We are together in our suffering.
We are together in our death.
We are divided by our achievements, our virtues, and our tri-
umphs.
But in our fear and our failure, our rage and our helplessness
    We are one.
We find our unity before your cross.
It belongs to all of us.
We are both the violating and the violated.
We are both the inflictors of pain and the bearers of pain.
We are the killers and the diers.
That is our common life, Lord.
Realizing who we are, those for whom you died,

we need no defense.
No excuses are necessary.
We can only say to you,
Lord have mercy,
Christ have Mercy,
Lord have Mercy.
We can only wait for the answer.

You asked us to return to Galilee and wait for you.
You have promised to come back to us.
"Go back to your fishing, your housekeeping, your farming.
Go back to your school and your loves and your dinner parties."
And there you will see me.
While we are breaking bread, our eyes will be opened,
    and we will know you are there.
While walking along together and talking with each other,
    you will come and walk beside us.
While we are pulling our fish into the boat,
    you will appear on the shore making breakfast for us.
Even when we are on the road to Damascus to persecute you
again, you will get through to us.
If we wait.

Teach us to care and not to care
Teach us to sit still
Even among these rocks,
Our peace in his will
And even among these rocks
Sister, mother
and spirit of the river, spirit of the sea,
Suffer me not to be separated

And let my cry come unto Thee.[1]

Lord have mercy
Christ have mercy
Lord have mercy.

III

REIGNING FROM THE TREE

The Passion According to St.John

As we read the story of Jesus' arrest, trial, and crucifixion in the Gospel according to St. John, we move into an atmosphere quite different from the atmosphere of Matthew, and Mark. The events seem to take place on a larger stage. The "majestic timelessness of divinity" stands forth more clearly. In the first three Gospels salvation is looked for in and through events in time. The Kingdom of God will come "on earth." God has acted and will act through historical events recognizable as part of the world of our ordinary experience. John illuminates his drama with light from another world. For him, this world co-exists with another, heavenly world. The meaning of our fallen history is not to be sought within the framework of time and recorded events, but rather through participation in an eternal realm which is always present above, below, and along side the life we know.

For John, writing after the fall of Jerusalem in 70 A.D., the fine points of historical distinctions have become relatively unimportant. The Pharisees, Zealots, tax-collectors, Herodians, who populated the Gospels have begun to disappear. In this Gospel there are only two kinds of people: those who come to the light that Jesus has brought into a world of darkness, and those who turn away from it. Everything is based on how one responds to Jesus the Eternal Word of God who has entered this realm from Eternity.

Those who rejected Jesus and sought his destruction are called "the Jews." By "the Jews" John meant the religious authorities who were hostile to Jesus. In reading his account it is easy to forget that most of the other characters were Jews, too: Jesus, Peter, Mary, all the disciples and followers of Jesus. John's use of the term "the Jews" to refer to the religious authorities hostile to Jesus, has been a major source of human tragedy and blot on Christian history we call anti-Semitism. Over the centuries, the reading of St. John's Gospel on Good Friday has undoubtedly helped to justify the persecution of generations of Jewish people. Christians moved by the sight of their Lord's execution have sought someone to blame for the death of the Son of God, lest they have to take the responsibility to themselves. Unfortunately, John's Gospel has been read in such a way as to put all the blame on a group of people who still do not accept Jesus as God's Word to them.

While reading the first three Gospels, we can easily understand the story as a human tragedy, and be touched, no matter what theological meaning we give it, by the human pathos and frailty and misunderstanding we see there. In John's account Jesus is less the helpless victim than the victorious conqueror. The crucifixion is not presented as the final defeat of Jesus' hopes, but as the final victory of this emissary from the Eternal World. He is always in control of the situation. He lays down his life voluntarily. He stands as the judge of his judges. By allowing himself to be lifted up on the cross, he draws all people to himself.

As we meditate on the events described in John, we are led to repentance, not because we identify with the weakness of the human characters around the cross, but because we are confronted by the God-Man. Our attention is not focused on the dying God deserted by his human friends, but on the central figure of the drama, the Jesus who will be glorified on the cross. Our reflection focuses not on our weakness, but on his strength.

He stands before us on the solid foundation of his relationship with the Eternal before whose glory the events of history, including his own suffering, are pale shadows. Before this figure we become aware of how overwhelming the threats to our life are and how easily lost we become in our darkness and our pain. Throughout St. John's passion narrative, Jesus shines as a light in the darkness which can never overcome it. He reigns from the tree. John sees the same events Matthew and Mark describe, but through a different lens, and he uses a different vocabulary. We are invited to see our days in the light of the Eternal Son of God who "was made flesh and dwelt among us, full of grace and truth," even, or especially, in his dying.

16

Who Is It You Want?

After these words, Jesus went out with his disciples, and crossed the Kedron ravine. There was a garden there, and he and his disciples went into it. The place was known to Judas, his betrayer, because Jesus had often met there with his disciples. So Judas took a detachment of soldiers, and police provided by the chief priests and the Pharisees, equipped with lanterns, torches, and weapons, and made his way to the garden. Jesus, knowing all that was coming upon him, went out to them and asked, "Who is it you want?" "Jesus of Nazareth," they answered. Jesus said, "I am he." And there stood Judas the traitor with them. When he said, "I am he," they drew back and fell to the ground. Again Jesus asked, "Who is it you want?" "Jesus of Nazareth," they answered. Then Jesus said, "I have told you that I am he. If I am the man you want, let these others go." (This was to make good his words, "I have not lost one of those whom thou gavest me.") Thereupon Simon Peter drew the sword he was wearing and struck at the High Priest's servant, cutting off his right ear. (The servant's name was Malchus.) Jesus said to Peter, "Sheathe your sword. This is the cup the Father has given me; shall I not drink it?"

(John 18: 1-11 NEB)

They came to arrest you,
this group of Roman soldiers and temple police.
They came looking for you in the dark
    with their lanterns
    and torches
    and weapons.
Boldened by their light
    and their weapons
    and their numbers
They expected you to run and hide among the bushes.
They expected to snare you in their net
    like a frightened animal.
The excitement of the chase drew them on.
But instead of a cringing animal
    they found *a man*.
    a man who stepped forward into their light
    and asked, "Who is it you want?"
Their warrant bore the name,
    "Jesus of Nazareth."
"I am he," you said.
And they fell to the ground.

What was the power in these words
    to make these armed hunters fall back?
When Moses stood before the bush that burned
    with the challenge to free his people,
He asked the voice from the bush its name,
And the voice replied, I AM
    That is who I am.
    Tell them, I AM has sent you.
"I am he," Jesus said.
    I am the one you are looking for.
The police and soldiers heard the divine name, "I AM."
Before that name, all people prostrate themselves.
That name holds within it the mystery of existence.

I AM—
>the One who causes things to be
>the One who lets things be
>The person of Being itself
>The power by which all things exist
>I AM

For just a moment, those who came to arrest you sensed they
were dealing with more than a cornered fanatic.
They encountered a man who stood forth in the power
>of the divine name.
For just a moment they saw who you really are.
For just a moment they knew who they were dealing with.
And they fell back in fear and awe.
But only for a moment.
Their vision of the mysterious presence flickered and was gone.
They reminded themselves that you were only a false prophet
>from an obscure village that they were looking for.
They were not looking for God.
They were not looking for the great I AM.

You let them off the hook.
You assured them you were the only one they wanted.
You used the power of the divine name to set
>free those who were with you.
You did not use it to defend yourself.
Your hour had come to return to the Father,
>and you expedited the business of that hour.
Your hour was at hand,
>the cup was ready and you took it up freely.
You were in charge, not the soldiers and police.
You knew what was going on, they did not.
You were the light in that darkness.
And so you let them bind you and arrest *you*
>the free one,
>the liberator of others.

You allowed yourself to be bound and arrested.
You the life-giver, went forth to die.
You ask us the same question
　all of us stumbling through the darkness
　with our lanterns and torches and weapons.
Whom are you looking for?
Who is it you want?
Whom seek ye?

Disturbing questions.
　Disturbing because honestly I don't know.
I am looking for something, for someone . . .
　But for whom? Or for what?
I feel powerless, weak, impotent.
　I am looking for someone who will be strong for me
　who will protect me
　who will be omnipotent for me.
I live in the shadow of death, my own death,
　and the death of my people and I look for
　someone to protect me from death.
I am looking amid the chaos of my world for structure
　and for order for someone to keep in line those forces
　within me and around me that threaten
　relapse into chaos.
　I am looking for someone to put the world right.
But you don't offer me that.

What you have to offer, you say, is water, living water.
　The water that I shall give . . . will be an inner spring,
always welling up for eternal life.[1]
　And bread. Living bread.
　The bread that God gives comes down from heaven and
brings life to the world.[2]

What you have to offer is light.
　I am the light of the world.[3]

The light shines on in the dark, and the darkness has never mastered it.[4]

I have come into this world — to give sight to the sightless and to make blind those who see.[5]

You offer life, eternal life.

If a man has faith in me, even though he die, he shall come to life.[6]

You ask me to look into the abyss
    and see there the loving arms of the Eternal Father,
    offering me companionship with the source
    and ground of existence.
You invite me to know
    and live in
    and draw power from
    the One who moves in all things and persons.
Who is it I want?
Who is it I seek when I seek you, Jesus of Nazareth?
    A Galilean prophet?
    Or more?
Is it the Father whom I seek?
    Yes, but more than that.
It is myself I am looking for.
    Who am *I*? What am *I*? What do *I* mean?
It is myself I need to know and understand and love.
I need to be able to say, I AM in the power
of the great I AM, to know
One who delights in me,
    and in the power of that relationship
    to delight in myself.
That is who I am looking for.

If you are the door,
    the way,
    the shepherd

who will lead me to that, Jesus, then indeed, you are
the one I am looking for.
Are you that way, Jesus of Nazareth?
Are you that truth,
    captive who uses the divine name?
Are you that life,
    man on the way to death?
If so, you are the one I seek.

You are the one I want.
You are the one I am looking for.

17

Are You Too One
of This Man's Disciples?

The troops with their commander, and the Jewish police, now arrested Jesus and secured him. They took him first to Annas. Annas was father-in-law of Caiaphas, the High Priest for that year — the same Caiaphas who had advised the Jews that it would be to their interest if one man died for the whole people.

Jesus was followed by Simon Peter and another disciple.

This disciple, who was acquainted with the High Priest, went with Jesus into the High Priest's courtyard, but Peter halted at the door outside. So the other disciple, the High Priest's acquaintance went out again and spoke to the woman at the door, and brought Peter in.

The maid on duty at the door said to Peter, "Are you another of this man's disciples?" "I am not," he said.

The servants and the police had made a charcoal fire, because it was cold, and were standing round it warming themselves.

And Peter too was standing with them, sharing the warmth.

The High Priest questioned Jesus about his disciples and about what he taught.

Jesus replied, "I have spoken openly to all the world; I have always taught in synagogue and in the temple, where all Jews congregate; I have said nothing in secret.

Why question me? Ask my hearers what I told them; they know what I said."

When he said this, one of the police who was standing next to him struck him on the face, exclaiming, "Is that the way to answer the High Priest?"

Jesus replied, "If I spoke amiss, state it in evidence; if I spoke well, why strike me?"

So Annas sent him bound to Caiaphas the High Priest.

Meanwhile Simon Peter stood warming himself. The others asked, "Are you another of his disciples?"

But he denied it: "I am not," he said.

One of the High Priest's servants, a relation of the man whose ear Peter had cut off, insisted, "Did I not see you with him in the garden?"

Peter denied again, and just then a cock crew.

(John 18: 12-27 NEB)

Jesus, you are majestic in your dignity.
Bound and helpless, your self-assurance before the authorities shocked them.
You should have been timid,
You should have been asking for mercy.
You should have assured your accusers there was some mistake.
Instead, you demand a hearing.
You demand that they produce witnesses.
You deny nothing.
Peter, on the other hand,
    denies everything.
"Are you too, one of his disciples?" they ask.
"No I am not," he says.

How would I answer that question?
I am not as sure of the answer as I used to be.
On Sundays I'm usually in church.
My children have all been baptized.

I try to be a good person.

I don't deliberately do things to hurt people.

During the week I work as an engineer for an aircraft company. To complete my engineering studies, I had to work full time while attending college for five years. Since getting my degree I have done well, and now lead a design group for an advanced re-entry system for missiles carrying nuclear warheads.

When I first started on this job, someone asked me,

"What do you think God wants you to do most of all?"

"Just what I am doing," I said, "to help build this missile to protect our country."

At the time I really believed that building deterrent weapons was holding off a hot war until cold war differences could be negotiated.

As long as the Russians were doing it, I really believed we had no choice.

But lately I have stopped believing it.

In our plant it's all "me and my project." It's empire building to become indispensable.

Patriotic philosophies about defending our country are really subordinated to winning contracts and working more overtime.

I saw violations of the test ban treaty when underground nuclear explosions were vented into the Nevada atmosphere. I know people who were trying to circumvent what good may come out of negotiations to stop the arms race.

I know that the more accurate bombs and greater warhead yields we are making are no longer simply retaliatory deterrents, they are first strike weapons.

If we make these things, eventually we are going to want to use them.

We have enough war heads to destroy the enemy many times. But the bureaucrats and the profit seekers undermine all attempts at arms reduction.

It is for power and for profit that we keep going.

My energy, my intelligence, my imagination is used to creating something I believe should never be used. I ought to quit, but I'm afraid to quit.

So I decided to work for peace in my spare time. Participating in public peace activities, I have met a lot of people who were jeopardizing their liberty to save us all from the impossible, possible war.

I admire these people, but I can't follow them. Most of them don't have families, and I do.

If only the F.B.I. would find me out and withdraw my clearance, the decision would be made for me. But they haven't tumbled. The decision is still mine.

I attended the trial of the Hickman Three in Honolulu. They poured their own blood over top secret electronic warfare files. They said:

> We pour out our blood in the name of the God of love, who lives now in the world in the maimed flesh of suffering people.
> We pour out our blood in the name of the human family under God, a global community created to live in peace, in brotherhood and sisterhood, a community of love which can become fully real only when we are willing to resist the shedding of others' blood by the giving of our own.

That reminded me of you, Jesus.

It also raised again for me the question: What am I doing, participating in a program of destruction and death that I can't get out of?

If I try to leave, I'll lose everything:

> Jobs, home, friends, reputation, a way of life which means security to me and my family.

Is it right for me to jeopardize my family because of my conscience?

But what are my responsibilities to the other families who are

suffering now, while we prosper, and who would be destroyed if
we use what I am making?
That responsibility is too much for me, Jesus. It was all right for
you, you were not a family man.

When my children were baptized, the priest asked me:
    Will you strive for justice and peace among all
    people, and respect the dignity of every human being?
"I will with God's help." was my answer.
I am asking for your help now, Jesus.
What shall I do?
When the question comes, "Are you too, this man's disciple?"
What do I answer?
If I say, Yes, I will lose a lot.
If I say, No, or maybe, or some times, or "in a way,"
    I can go on as I am, but I will lose everything.
Lord, I don't know whose disciple I am.
You are so sure about who you are.
How can you be so sure?
You know what you are doing, Lord.
But what am I doing?

18

My Kingdom Does Not Belong to This World

From Caiaphas Jesus was led into the Governor's headquarters. It was now early morning, and the Jews themselves stayed outside the headquarters to avoid defilement, so that they could eat the Passover meal. So Pilate went out to them and asked, "What charge do you bring against this man?"

"If he were not a criminal," they replied, "We should not have brought him before you."

Pilate said, "Take him away and try him by your own law."

The Jews answered, "We are not allowed to put any man to death."

Thus they ensured the fulfillment of the words by which Jesus had indicated the manner of his death.

Pilate then went back into his headquarters and summoned Jesus.

"Are you the king of the Jews?" he asked.

Jesus said, "Is that your own idea, or have others suggested it to you?"

"What! am I a Jew?" said Pilate. "Your own nation and their chief priests have brought you before me. What have you done?"

Jesus replied, "My kingdom does not belong to this world. If it did, my followers would be fighting to save me from arrest by the Jews. My kingly authority comes from elsewhere."

"You are a king, then?" said Pilate.

Jesus answered, "'King' is your word. My task is to bear witness to the truth. For this was I born; for this I came into the world, and all who are not deaf to truth listen to my voice."

Pilate said, "What is truth?" and with these words went out again to the Jews.

"For my part," he said, "I find no case against him. But you have a custom that I release one prisoner for you at Passover. Would you like me to release the king of the Jews?"

Again the clamor rose, "Not him; we want Barabbas!"

(Barabbas was a bandit.)

(John 18:28-40 NEB)

Your Kingdom was not like a kingdom of this world.
In the kingdoms of this world, subjects fight to save their kings.
Your friends were not fighting.
By this statement you clearly separated yourself from the Zealots of your time, and of every time.
Your statement seemed to satisfy Pilate that you were innocent of the political charges.
Gods and philosophies, even miracles and healings, were none of his concern.
His only questions were,
> How many swords?
> How many guns?
> How many atomic bombs?
> How much oil?
> Are you for my interests
> > or are you a threat to my interests?
That's what counted in Pilate's scheme of things.
Whatever power you had, would make no difference in his world.
Your kingship had nothing to do with

armies and courts,
    with justice and injustice
    with bread or scarcity
    with democracy or dictatorship
Or so it seemed to Pilate.

But Lord, there are things to be done in this world
    wrongs to be righted,
    evils to be resisted,
    disasters to be avoided
And they all call for the use of power.
What happens to people in this world is important.
You know that.
    You fed the hungry.
    You healed the sick.
    You drove the demons out.
    You cleansed the temple.
Your Father's Kingdom was coming. You said it was coming
soon, it was coming here, and the things you did were a sign of
its coming.
Now you stand with your hands tied behind you
    and say your Kingdom is not of this world.
It *must* matter to you that people be fed.
It *must* matter to you that the water and the land and the at-
    mosphere be preserved for future generations.
It *must* matter to you that people have
    the freedom to direct their own lives.
We have to fight for these things.
We have to fight for food
    for the biosphere
    for freedom.
You just can't mean what happens in this world doesn't matter.
To do anything about hunger, or ecology, or freedom
    means using force and power.
Change doesn't happen without the use of power.

If your followers simply sit on their hands and meditate
    on the Kingdom of God within them,
    they will be assisting the forces of evil and oppression.
We have to think about the rule of God out there in the factories
    in the parliaments
    in the laboratories
    in the forests.
As soon as we take this world's problems seriously we are going
to have to fight.

We are going to have to fight the people who are causing other
people to starve.
We are going to have to fight the people who are destroying the
earth.
We are going to have to fight those who are taking away other
people's freedom.
We are going to have enemies.

You say "My Kingdom is not of this world"?
Do you want us to ignore the power of evil and leave everything
to God to straighten out?
If that's what you meant, your followers have not followed you.
We have not been willing to leave the issue to the One you say
holds the whole world in his hands.
We have made his cause, our cause, his right, our right,
his hope for the world, our hopes for the world.
Or have we turned it around and called our kingdom your King-
dom?

Our faith in you, we said, led us to mount crusades against the
infidels.
Declaring the earth is the Lord's, we decided He had given it to
his saints and that we are the saints, so we could take it from the
Indians in good conscience.
Because we believed our ways were your ways, we destroyed ancient cultures and ancient customs in the name of your cross.

In the name of your freedom, we have bombed and burned and exiled people we did not understand.

To preserve the free world, we have tolerated torture and violence.

Because we believe in God, and our enemies don't, we say we are building nuclear bombs and aiming them at our enemy whom we call your enemy.

Since we think we know what your Kingdom in this world would look like, we have improved on your method.

We have joined the Zealots in the use of force.

But you stand before us, facing what looks like the failure of your earthly mission and you say there is One whose purposes transcend every human purpose, One who even uses your enemies in the fulfillment of his designs.

You leave your cause in his hands and refuse to make even your own safety an absolute.

Even *your* cause does not justify violence.

Even *your* cause is not the measure of all things. For us, those who disagree with our good become evil.

Our devotion, and fervor in the pursuit of our righteous causes leads us to massacres, exploitations, oppression, torture, detainment camps.

Oh Jesus, free us from the tyranny of our great causes,
>   our sacred beliefs
>   our all encompassing ideologies.

Can you help us stand in the power of a truth that need not resort to victory?

Can you teach us that we do not prove our God is stronger than other gods by beating up those who disagree with us? You came into this world from your Father and took its pains and problems with absolute seriousness. But you did not take your own success, your own survival, your own cause with absolute seriousness.

Give us an anchor in One who is not of this world, so that we may participate in the causes of this world without fanaticism. Show us the signs of your rule in this world and empower us to commit ourselves to those signs, but keep us open to the possibility, that our good is not your good.

Prepare us to expect surprises.

Set us against all absolute ideologies: Marxism, Maoism, Liberal Democracy, Capitalism, Socialism, Me-first-ism.

Show us how to work and fight and strive as those who are rooted and grounded in a Kingdom which is not of this world.

✳ 19

Where Have You Come from?

Once more Pilate came out and said to the Jews, "Here he is; I am bringing him out to let you know that I find no case against him"; and Jesus came out, wearing the crown of thorns and the purple cloak.

"Behold the Man!" said Pilate.

The chief priests and their henchmen saw him and shouted, "Crucify! Crucify!"

"Take him and crucify him yourselves," said Pilate; "for my part I find no case against him."

The Jews answered, "We have a law; and by that law he ought to die, because he has claimed to be the Son of God."

When Pilate heard that, he was more afraid than ever, and going back into his headquarters he asked Jesus,

"Where have you come from?"

But Jesus gave him no answer.

"Do you refuse to speak to me?" said Pilate.

"Surely you know that I have authority to release you, and I have authority to crucify you?"

"You would have no authority at all over me," Jesus replied, "if it had not been granted you from above; and therefore the deeper guilt lies with the man who handed me over to you."

From that moment Pilate tried hard to release him; but the Jews kept shouting, "If you let this man go, you are no friend of Caesar; any man who claims to be a king is defying Caesar."

When Pilate heard what they were saying, he brought Jesus

out and took his seat at the tribunal at the place known as "The
Pavement" ("Gabbatha" in the language of the Jews).

It was the eve of Passover, about noon.

Pilate said to the Jews, "Here is your king."

They shouted, "Away with him! Away with him! Crucify
him!"

"Crucify your king?" said Pilate.

"We have no king but Caesar," the Jews replied.

Then at last, to satisfy them, he handed Jesus over to be crucified.

(John 19: 4–16 NEB)

Pilate, the man who was supposed to have authority
>   to judge you
>   to crucify you
>   to release you
could not do what he wanted to do.
Pilate, who did not pretend to know about truth —
>   your truth
>   or the Jews' truth,
>   but only about political power and necessity,
Pilate was caught in a trap.
He had called you innocent and no political threat to him.
He mockingly crowned you with thorns
>   and robed you in purple,
>   and brought you forth to those who sought your life.
>   "Look at this poor fellow," he said.
>   Behold the man.
>   Isn't it ridiculous to take such a figure seriously?
>   Perhaps by your lights he is a false prophet.
So I have had him beaten and humiliated for his pretension.
That's enough. I'll let him go.
He's harmless.
Let's be done with this.
But then the religious leaders brought out their most important
charge.

They said you claimed to be God's son.

That was blasphemy and deserving of death.

No one should be allowed to make himself one with the transcendent holy whose name was too awful to pronounce.

And you had said,

> "I and the Father are One.
>
> He who has seen me has seen the Father.
>
> Unless you believe that I am in the Father and the Father in me, you are children of darkness."

Your offense to your accuser was not political, it was religious.

You were blasphemous.

No wonder Pilate was afraid.

A political charge could be dealt with pragmatically,

> sensibly, rationally.

But now, he was afraid, political reason would not prevail.

Religious reasons are not subject to argument or negotiation.

Pilate knew he would never shake their fanatical determination born of religious faith.

What could he do now?

He believed neither in your truth or their truth.

He wanted to be a reasonable man, but he also had to make clear, or pretend, that he was in charge, that he was the authority here.

He had told you that life and death were in his hands.

You told him he was only a tool of God, given an unwitting role to play in a cosmic drama being written from above.

Pilate was not the final authority here, because your enemies had power over him, because he was vulnerable to political blackmail.

He had bet his life and future on keeping Caesar's trust.

If he now let a pretender "king" go free, he gave his enemies a weapon to use against him.

They had finally found Pilate's vulnerable point.

His future was in their hands, too.

In desperation he asks you,

> "Where have you come from?"

Do you come from Nazareth?

Are you simply the beaten man standing before me?

Or is there more to you?

Do you have powers of occult origin?

He sensed your authority even more as he began to doubt his own.

Where did you get it?

Where have you come from?

You do not answer.

But you tell him that what authority he has comes from "above."

You know the source of his power, and of all power,

His power, all power, comes from above — from your Father.

You do not say so, but it is clear that your power also comes from above.

You are the true son of the Father, the true Bar-Abbas.

By charging you with blasphemy, your accusers have raised the ante for Pilate, for he is required to support the religious customs of his subjects.

It is easy for him to deal with you as a political threat, but the claim of divine sonship —

that is too prickly and uncertain for such a pragmatic man.

Fired with religious fervor your enemies would never be satisfied with a simple beating. They will insist on crucifixion.

Pilate has to let the drama, the divine drama, go on.

He has to let you be lifted up

so that the whole world can be drawn to you.

The irony of it.

Pilate speaks the truth.

He calls you a King.

He says you are The Man.

He pronounces you innocent.

He does not know what he is saying.

He does not see the truth he speaks.

But he does not stand in the way

of your final hour,
of your final triumph.
He steps aside, and lets you be crucified.

"Look at the man," Pilate says.
What do I see when I look at you,
    Jesus of Nazareth?
I certainly don't see a Superman.
    Superman is invulnerable.
Superman's power comes from above too,
    but if he involves himself in human love on this planet,
    he becomes vulnerable to human pains and loses his power.
You stand with blood running down your face ready to embrace
the whole world — vulnerable.
Most powerful when most vulnerable.
When I look at you Jesus of Nazareth,
    I see a human being with hopes, fears, loves.
    I see a human animal with capacity for pain.
    I see a human life
        moving from childhood's helplessness
        to the helplessness of the executed.
        You are no Superman.
But you are a man.
You stand with dignity before your accusers.
You speak with your judge as one having authority.
Where do you come from?
    You come from your mother's womb.
    You come from growing up in Nazareth working in your
father's shop.
    You come from synagogue and from temple.
    You come from an ancient people with a promise.
    You come from among the followers of John the Baptist.
    You come from climbing the hills of Galilee and the moun-
tain to Jerusalem.
    You come from the seashore and from the dinner party.
    You come from all the places I come from.

But they say you pretended to be God's Son.
Were they not right in condemning you for this,
    Jesus of Nazareth?
For if you asked us to worship you as a man,
    you would have blasphemed against the One, the Eternal
God.
    He does not live in temples made by men and women.
    He does not live in bodies made by men and women.
    He dwells in a high and Holy Place.
To claim to be His son is an offense
    against the purest and highest religious sentiments.
Your people dared not mention the divine name,
    how could they worship a human being?

I too am afraid of this kind of talk.
I do not want to be tied to a God who appears in
    one place and not in others.
I want a God I can meet anywhere and everywhere.
If I accept this claim made by you,
    I would have to take you
    and your words
    and your life and death
more seriously than any other words or life or death
    including my own.
If I really believed that you came from above
    that you were God's beachhead in this world,
    it would turn my world upside down.
It would call for a commitment and a trust
    that I'm not ready to give.
It would mean trusting you as the ultimate clue
    to the deepest reality of this life.
It would mean living in your truth, your way, your life.
    I am not sure I am ready for that.
"How could the Eternal do a temporal act,
    the Infinite become a finite fact?"
I would like to remain neutral, like Pilate.

I would like to reduce your claim to something I can manage or
dismiss.
Stay as Jesus of Nazareth—
Or reveal yourself as Superman.
Don't ask me to trust the divine in a human form.
I'm too sophisticated for that.
You are truly man.
Are you truly God?
That kind of talk makes me afraid, too.
I don't want to decide. I am just an observer here.

Leave me alone.
Leave me.
Leave.

* **20**

It Is Finished

So they took Jesus, and he went out, bearing his own cross, to the place called the place of a skull, which is called in Hebrew Golgotha. There they crucified him, and with two others, one on either side, and Jesus between them. Pilate also wrote a title and put it on the cross; it read, "Jesus of Nazareth, the King of the Jews." Many of the Jews read this title, for the place where Jesus was crucified was near the city; and it was written in Hebrew, in Latin, and in Greek. The chief priests of the Jews then said to Pilate, "Do not write, 'The King of the Jews,' but, 'This man said, I am the King of the Jews.'" Pilate answered, "What I have written I have written."

When the soldiers had crucified Jesus, they took his garments and made four parts, one for each soldier. But his tunic was without seam, woven from top to bottom; so they said to one another, "Let us not tear it, but cast lots for it to see whose it shall be." This was to fulfil the scripture.

> "They parted my garments among them,
> and for my clothing they cast lots."

So the soldiers did this; but standing by the cross of Jesus were his mother, and his mother's sister, Mary the wife of Clopas, and Mary Magdalene. When Jesus saw his mother, and the disciple whom he loved standing near, he said to his mother, "Woman, behold your son!" Then he said to the disciple, "Behold your-mother!" And from that hour the disciple took her to his own home.

After this Jesus, knowing that all was now finished, said (to fulfil the scripture), "I thirst." A bowl full of vinegar stood there; so they put a sponge full of the vinegar on hyssop and held it to his mouth. When Jesus had received the vinegar, he said, "It is finished"; and he bowed his head and gave up his spirit.

(John 19:17–30 RSV)

It is finished.

Your last words are often on our lips, Lord.

My friend Bob came to talk about his marriage.

It is breaking up. It is finished, he said.

I asked my friend who was writing a book how it was going.

It is finished, he said.

I can say "It is finished" with great satisfaction, or with great despair.

When the music is over, the play is over, I say, "It is finished."

When something I had hoped would last comes to a bad end, I say, "It is finished" with sadness.

It is finished can mean simply "It is over," or it can mean, "It is completed." It makes a great deal of difference which you mean.

Sam Keen spoke of his father's death at an advanced age, "He died only at the end of his life." He meant that he did not die *before* the end of his life, and that when he died his life was complete.

What did you mean Lord? Did you mean your life was complete, or that it was simply over. The Gospel says you knew that all had come to its appointed end. You had lived the way you wanted to live. You had completed your mission. "It is finished" for you meant, "It is complete." It meant you had lived the truth you wanted to live to the end. It meant you were satisfied. Your life was not a defeat, but a victory. When I think about my own death, it is important to know whether "It is finished" will mean simply that it is over, or whether it will mean, "It is complete."

You died very young

A sense of completeness doesn't depend on many, many years. One of the most helpful things that came to me when my wife died was a note from a friend of hers who wrote:

> How good for us to know and for her to have known that she lived in fulfillment. By that I mean that she suffered, was angered, felt desire, and joy, attained fruition, made mistakes, fought for change, had successes, knew her own faults and did not find herself alone.
>
> The saddest death of all is one in which the person has never really lived and never experienced the fullness of which human beings are capable.

The worst thing about death is the feeling that you never really lived.

Worst of all is to feel you have missed it. That you were somehow deprived of what life promised.

The worst thing is to face your death, only with the feeling that "Time's Up," your opportunities have ended, and you have missed it.

If I knew that I was to die tomorrow, what would I mourn most? One of the astronauts wrote to his wife before his flight. "If this venture comes to a flaming end, I will have to regret not living to love you as a grandmother and never learning to play the guitar really well."

What possibility will I have not claimed?

What good will I have missed?

Will I be angry about all the things I didn't do?

Or will I be able to say, "It is finished. It is complete.

It has been good. I am satisfied. It meant something that I lived."

I'm not sure how I will answer that question.

Is it too late to reorder my priorities?
Is it too late to change my patterns?
Is it too late to open up new horizons?

Lord, as you laid down your life you knew that you had done what you came into this world to do.
O Lord, help me live now so that when I come to my end, I will be able to say, "It is finished," and mean, "It is complete."

21

Look on Him Whom They Have Pierced

Because it was the eve of Passover, the Jews were anxious that the bodies should not remain on the cross for the coming Sabbath, since that Sabbath was a day of great solemnity; so they requested Pilate to have the legs broken and the bodies taken down. The soldiers accordingly came to the first of his fellow-victims and to the second, and broke their legs; but when they came to Jesus, they found that he was already dead, so they did not break his legs. But one of the soldiers stabbed his side with a lance, and at once there was a flow of blood and water. This is vouched for by an eyewitness, whose evidence is to be trusted. He knows that he speaks the truth, so that you too may believe; for this happened in fulfillment of the text of Scripture: "No bone of his shall be broken." And another text says, "They shall look on him whom they pierced."

(John 19:31-37 NEB)

> Upon the cross of Jesus, mine eyes at times can see
> The very dying form of one who suffered there for me.
> And from my smitten heart with tears,
> Two wonders I confess
> The wonders of redeeming love, and my own
> worthlessness.[1]

I watch you live out your vocation
    to the end.
You were called to open our eyes to see the Father.
You were called to be an intersection
    of his timelessness
    with our time.
You were called to show forth
    an infinite glory
    in a finite life.
You were called to lay down your life
    that from its ashes
    new life might spring up for many and for me.
You were called to gather a new community,
    filled with spirit,
    to share in God's suffering for the fulfillment
    of the whole creation.
You were raised up on the cross
    to draw all of us into your vocation.
    to enable all of us to find
    the meaning of our beginning and our end
    through the prism of your life and death and resurrection.

I have stood before your cross and watched you
I have stood before your cross and looked at myself.
When I see you do not hesitate to affirm your ground in the
great I AM my cowardice and uncertainty become apparent.
If only I could be as sure who I am as you are sure.
When I see that you know why you are here
    and whose truth you are to be;
When I see you care about those the Father has given you
    to the very end;
When I see that your self-concern never takes over—
    My commitment
    to those you have given to me,
    is revealed as half-hearted,

temporary,
and pro-tem.
I see how I limit my liabilities, how I protect myself.
When I observe that you do not use your power to overwhelm,
to control, to destroy—
When I observe you turn your back on all power games;
When I observe you remain loyal to the transcendent vision
even in your jeopardy;
When I observe you standing free of the passions of this world,
sustained by a reality not of this world—
My need to control stands out in dark relief.

I observe how my devotion to my good turns into hatred of
any who resist me, and turns those who disagree into evil people.
I hear my voice as one more cry of "Crucify!"
I see myself out of touch with the unseen power
who shapes the destiny of all, forgetful of the dark side of
my ambition.
How sure you are that the eternal from which you came calls
you to suffer here!
How sure you are that you can trust One who calls you from on
high!
You come from Nazareth—do you also come out of the mystery
of God?

It puzzles me that "infinite can be a finite fact."
I do not want to believe it.
I do not want to take any one thing in this world that seriously,
I look for the eternal in splendid things—
in rapture,
in the grand sweep,
in a universal truth, discoverable anywhere.
not in any human thing, any small thing—
not in a peasant from Galilee,
not in flesh and blood . . .
I want a spirit, free, expansive, unlimited, untied down.

I watch you completing your life
offering it up when the job is finished.
I watch you giving your life so that others might live.
Myself, I can't believe I will ever die.
Tomorrow is soon enough to begin to live.
But your job is finished.
It is all over.
You are dead.
They poke your side
to make sure you are dead.
And from your lifeless body
pours forth water
and blood.
Yours is not the only blood being shed that day.
While you are dying outside the city on a cross, the priests are
busy at work in the temple.
They are slaughtering the lambs in preparation for the feast of
Passover.
They are draining the blood from the lambs to sprinkle it over
the worshippers, to wash away their impurity, to prepare them
to approach the Holy God.
Their ancestors had sprinkled the blood on the doors of their
houses in Egypt on the night when the great I AM led them out
of slavery. The blood sprinkled on the doorpost identified them
as no longer slaves but a people called to be God's people in the
world.
The death of the lambs was the beginning of a new creation,
and birth of a royal priesthood, a holy nation.
The life of the lamb, the death of the lamb,
was a sign of new life offered to the Eternal Life and
made Eternal Life available to them.
The lambs were dying again
to celebrate the gift of freedom
the gift of life to a particular people.
Your life was being offered

to set all people free
to open the life of the Eternal to all.
You were the Lamb of God.
Your spirit was set loose to enliven everyone.
The water from your side became a river,
    a red sea, an ocean that would cleanse all who entered it.
It was living water, the water of life.
Those who entered it,
    those who drank of it,
    those who were cleansed by it,
would be your people.
    They would never thirst again,
    they would never be unclean again,
    they would be nurtured by life-giving water.
My baptism in your water, and in your blood is the passageway
into a new freedom.
The vitality of your life
    flowing out of your side,
    your blood, sprinkled on me, incorporates me into a new
people
    a people fed in the wilderness
    a people called to freedom
    a people called to participate in God's suffering
    for the whole world.
I know life has come from your death
    It is the life I live,
    My food and drink. My cleansing. My hope. Thanks be to
God.

IV

EPILOGUE

Recalling His Death, Resurrection and Ascension, We Offer You These Gifts . . .

The end of John's passion points to the creation of a new people sustained by the water of baptism, and the blood of the new covenant. Our life in the Church begins with our passage through the water, and continues as we drink the cup of his blood "for the remembrance of him" . . . bringing him into our present, so that we may encounter over and over again the one who comes out of the mystery of suffering offering us his peace. We see him and we don't see him. We reach out to him. He reaches out to us, and from the mutual touching our life touches the mystery of the God who came to "share our human nature, to live and die as one of us, to reconcile us to [himself], the God and Father of All."

The essence of this drama, and its reenactment in gatherings of Christians is described poignantly by Alan Paton in his "Meditation for a Young Boy Confirmed."

Such was the brief, such was the lonely life,
Such was the bondage of the earth, such was the misery,
Such was the reaching out, such was the separation,
That my Lord tore the curtain from the skies, and in compassion
He took upon Himself all angry things, the scourge,
the thorn, the nail,
    the utter separation;

And spoke such words as made me tremble, and laid
    His yoke upon me
And bound me with these chains, that I have worn
    with no especial grace.
Why then did I accept this miracle, and being what I am
    some lesser miracles,
And then I did accept this Faith, and being what I am
    some certain Articles,
And then I did accept this Law, and being what I am
    some regulations,
Why then I worshiped Him, and being what I am
    knelt in some pew
And heard some organ play and some bells peal,
    and heard some people sing,
And heard about some money that was wanted, and
    heard some sin was preached against,
And heard some message given by some man, sometimes
    with great distinction, sometimes none.
I made this humble access, I too stretched out my hands,
Sometimes I saw Him not, and sometimes clearly,
    though with my inward eyes.
I stayed there on my knees, I saw His feet approaching,
I saw the mark of the nails, I did not dare to look fully at them
I longed to behold Him, I did not care to behold Him,
I said in my heart to Him, I who in sins and doubts and
    in my grievous separation reach out my hands,
Reach out Thy hands and touch me, oh most Holy One.[1]

Notes

Preface
1. Jürgen Moltmann, *The Crucified God* (New York: Harper and Row, 1973).
2. Raymond E. Brown, *The Anchor Bible: The Gospel according to John* (New York: Doubleday and Co., Inc., 1966).

2 *A Blasphemous Healer*
1. W.H. Auden, "For the Time Being: A Christmas Oratorio," *Collected Longer Poems* (New York: Random House, 1934), pp. 187, 189, 190.

4 *The God Forsaken God*
1. Elie Wiesel, *Night* (New York: Hill and Wang, 1960), pp. 70f.

5 *The Challenge of the Innocent Victim*
1. Albert Camus, *The Plague* (New York: Random House, 1948), p. 89.
2. Ibid. pp. 90–91.
3. Ibid. p. 201.
4. Ibid. p. 203.
5. Ibid. p. 211.

II   **To Share His Suffering**
1. A collect for Fridays, *Book of Common Prayer* (New York: The Seabury Press, 1977), p. 99.

15 *Lord Have Mercy*
1. "Ash Wednesday," T.S. Eliot, *The Complete Poems and Plays* (New York: Harcourt, Brace & World, 1971), pp. 61, 67.

16 *Who Is It You Want?*
1. John 4:14 NEB.
2. John 6:33 NEB.
3. John 8:12 NEB.
4. John 1:5 NEB.
5. John 9:39 NEB.
6. John 11:25 NEB.

21 *Look on Him Whom They Have Pierced*
1. Hymn 341, *The Hymnal of the Protestant Episcopal Church* (New York: The Seabury Press, 1940).

IV   **Epilogue**
1. "Meditation for a Young Boy Confirmed," Alan Paton, *The Advent Papers* (Cincinnati, Ohio: Forward Movement Publications).